INSIGHT POCKET GUIDE

Hanoi
& NORTHERN VIETNAM

Discovery
CHANNEL

APA PUBLICATIONS
Part of the Langenscheidt Publishing Group

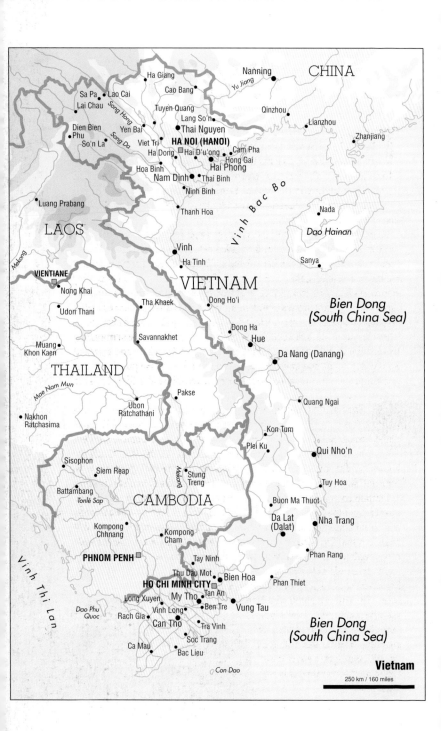

Vietnam

250 km / 160 miles

Welcome

This guidebook combines the interests and enthusiasms of two of the world's best-known information providers: Insight Guides, who have set the standard for visual travel guides since 1970, and Discovery Channel, the world's premier source of non-fiction television programming. Its aim is to bring you the best of Hanoi city and its surroundings in a series of tailor-made itineraries devised by Insight's Vietnam-based correspondent, Samantha Coomber.

Hanoi has witnessed a turbulent history stretching back a millennia and has served as the capital of the first independent Vietnamese state, French Indochina and, now, of a united Vietnam. The first three itineraries present the city's essential sights, including the Old Quarter, with its fascinating warren of streets, and the much-revered Ho Chi Minh Mausoleum. Six optional itineraries – ranging from a craft tour to Vietnamese cooking classes – offer both half- and full-day tours focusing on Hanoi's rich and varied heritage.

For visitors with more time, six excursions venture out to the surrounding region with its beautiful pagodas, breathtaking Halong Bay and highland Sapa. Chapters on shopping, eating out and nightlife, plus a practical information section covering travel essentials complete this reader-friendly guide.

 Samantha Coomber is an English freelance travel writer who first visited Vietnam in 1998 – after a working stint in the UK travel trade. She has travelled extensively throughout the country, off the beaten track and where few foreigners venture. Based in Hanoi she knows the city in depth and has worked on a number of guidebooks to Vietnam. She is currently the writer and editor for a national tourist magazine.

Despite encroaching urbanization, Hanoi is still a charming city with a unique small-town feel. Visitors will sense Hanoi's momentous past through its rich cultural and architectural fabric, and at the same time, witness the first chaotic, stumbling steps the city is taking towards modernisation. In spite of its tragic past and Socialist ideology, the capital can be a fun and friendly city with an 'almost anything is possible' atmosphere. As Samantha says, 'After several years of living here, I am still not bored with Hanoi – you never quite get to totally unravel its multi-layered complexities and nuances.' Hanoi, she enthuses, 'should come with a government health alert – warning: this city is addictive!'

HISTORY AND CULTURE

For over 1,000 years Hanoi has been at the centre of Vietnam's turbulent and fascinating history, imprints of which have been indelibly stamped on it......................**11**

CITY ITINERARIES

The first three full-day itineraries cover Hanoi's essential sights, and include recommendations for meals en route. The remaining six tours – comprising half- and full-day options – explore selected aspects of the city and its immediate surroundings.

EXCURSIONS

A selection of day trips and short excursions explore the multi-faceted Northern Vietnam area.

LEISURE ACTIVITIES

CALENDAR OF EVENTS

PRACTICAL INFORMATION

MAPS

INDEX AND CREDITS

Pages 2/3: lotus-filled pond at Thay Pagoda complex
Pages 8/9: soldiers at Hanoi's Museum of Vietnamese Revolution

History & Culture

W hen Nam Viet became a Chinese protectorate in 111BC, the stage was set for a millennium of Chinese political and cultural dominance over present-day North Vietnam – and a depressing recurrence of wars and occupation which only ceased in 1979. Foreign aggressors, however, hadn't reckoned on the fierce determination of the North Vietnamese, which has more heroes than you can shake a stick at. Never forgotten, many of them live on for eternity in Hanoi's street names, ironically juxtaposed next to the unmistakable traces of foreign occupation.

The Chinese Spectre

In a pattern to repeat itself throughout history, efforts by the Chinese to assimilate the Vietnamese were met with fierce resistance, shaping the national identity. The two Trung sisters led Vietnam's first independence movement (AD40–43). Chinese forces overwhelmed the heroines and their modest army, but rather than surrender, the sisters threw themselves into the Red River.

When General Ngo Quyen defeated Chinese forces in 938 by way of stakes embedded in the Bach Dang River, it was the beginning of the end of Chinese rule over Annam ('the Pacified South'), establishing the first independent Vietnamese state. Ly Thai To, the founding king of the Ly Dynasty, which ruled over the North Vietnam kingdom of Dai Viet ('Great Viet') from the 11th to the 13th centuries, moved the capital to Dai La in 1010 after seeing an apparition of a golden dragon soar into the sky. He renamed it Thang Long ('city of the ascending dragon') – present-day Hanoi.

Buddhism flourished as the national religion, with numerous pagodas built during this period. Dykes and canals were constructed and a royal citadel was built on top of the former fortress. In the 13th century, small hamlets developed outside its walls, with craftsmen from the same guilds congregating to make and sell wares. Known as the Old Quarter, traces of this old geography are still visible today, in street names indicating specific merchandise (*hang*). Courts and government systems, however, were still modelled on Confucian philosophy. The Temple of Literature (Van Mieu) – founded in 1070 – became the nation's first university. The Vietnamese mandarin system of government evolved, with Van Mieu emerging as the mandarins' intellectual and spiritual centre.

The north experienced an almost unbroken period of independence, lasting well into the 19th century. The Chinese didn't stop attacking Dai Viet, but some of Vietnam's greatest

Left: a Vietnam War veteran
Right: gate at Hanoi's Temple of Literature

heroes managed to repel them. General Ly Thuong Kiet (1030–1105) led two successful attacks against the Sung (Chinese) forces during the Ly Dynasty. General Tran Hung Dao outfoxed Kublai Khan's Mongolian forces in 1285 and famously in 1288 at Bach Dang River (*see page 70*). A brief Ming Dynasty occupation (1407–27) saw many of the city's cultural, religious and historical works burned or taken to China. Another national hero emerged – Le Loi – who waged a guerilla war against the enemy. After his victory over the Chinese in 1428, Le Loi declared himself as Emperor Le Thai To, founded the Le Dynasty and renamed the capital Dong Kinh (later corrupted by the French as 'Tonkin'), restoring the city to its glory once more.

A Chinese invasion of another sort started in the 17th century when Chinese merchants settled in Dong Kinh: by the end of the 19th century, one quarter of the capital's inhabitants were of Chinese origin. However, at the same time the seeds were being sown for another chapter of foreign aggression, with the arrival of European missionaries from the 16th century onwards.

Emergence of Viet Nam

Prince Nguyen Phuc Anh (a member of one of the two royal clans ruling the country) declared himself as Emperor Gia Long in 1802, founding the Nguyen Dynasty, which lasted until 1945. He unified the country as Viet Nam ('the people of the south') and moved the capital to Hué. Dong Kinh – renamed Ha Noi ('city in the bend of the river') – was relegated to a regional capital and a smaller citadel was constructed on the old citadel's foundations.

The emperor's ascension and success over a peasant uprising led by the Tay Son brothers was aided by French missionary Pigneau de Behaine, who offered military aid in exchange for French commercial privileges. Although indebted to the French, Gia Long was suspicious of their motives. And rightly so: France was keen to colonise Vietnam and control the gateway to China. In the meantime, French missionaries poured into Viet Nam in large numbers. The French cited attacks on the French missionaries from the

Above: mandarin and escorts in Tonkin (North Vietnam)
Right: Ho Chi Minh in the field during the early 1950s

1820s onwards as a pretext for military intervention. The capture of Danang and Saigon, followed by Cochin China (South Vietnam) in the mid-19th century, heralded a colonial occupation lasting almost a century.

French Indochina rule

The French extended their control to the north in 1883. Annam (Central) and Tonkin (North) became French protectorates, combining with Cochin China to form French Indochina (present-day Vietnam, Cambodia and Laos) in 1887, making Hanoi its capital. When Hanoi fell into French hands, the city underwent a transformation – particularly in the 1890s. A new town along European lines was laid out around the old one. Marshland, swamps and lakes were drained and land was reclaimed for wide, tree-lined boulevards, parks and elegant buildings – including the present-day Government Guesthouse, Opera House and Sofitel Metropole Hotel. The 'little Paris of the Tropics' conjured up a reassuring image of home for French residents.

In the wake of progress, however, tradition suffered. Bao Tien Pagoda was pulled down to make way for St Joseph's Cathedral and Bao An Pagoda was replaced by the GPO. The Citadel was destroyed by French troops: today, only the Cot Co Flag Tower, North Gate, South Gate, Kinh Thien Palace and Ladies' Pagoda stand – some of which are undergoing renovations. The price of colonial rule was high. Women and children were recruited by French agents to work in mines and plantations. France looked to Indochina and Vietnam to supply 50,000 soldiers and as many workers to serve on the battlefields of World War I. Heavy taxes were levied on the people and construction of the Haiphong railway line cost the lives of 25,000 Vietnamese.

Rise of the Communist Party

Throughout the colonial period, the Vietnamese retained a strong sense of national identity. Fragmented uprisings were met with executions and imprisonment; many patriots and revolutionaries were incarcerated in Hanoi's Hoa Lo Prison. But this era saw the development of new radical groups, the beginnings of Vietnam's independence movement and the emergence of the greatest hero of them all – Nguyen Ai Quoc.

While wandering the world, a young Vietnamese revolutionary, Nguyen Ai Quoc, better known as Ho Chi Minh, developed a strong sense of political consciousness. While in Paris during the 1919 Versailles Peace Conference, he tried to petition US President Wilson with a plan for an independent Vietnam – Wilson refused to meet him. In his role as an international Communist agent, Ho founded the Indochinese Communist Party in Guangzhou, China, in 1930.

Meanwhile, Hanoi's Old Quarter was a key area for the growth of the Vietnamese patriotic movement. In 1929 the first Communist cell was founded, and during the 1930s many houses served as secret residences, workplaces and meeting places for a variety of patriotic organisations, including the Red Trade Unions and Communist Party of Hanoi.

World War II

World War II was a chaotic period in North Vietnam. The pro-Nazi Vichy government of France accepted the Japanese occupation of Indochina, but continued administering Vietnam. After 30 years in self-exile, Ho Chi Minh walked across the border into Vietnam in 1941 and co-founded the League for the Independence of Vietnam (Viet Minh). Its goal was not only independence from French colonial rule and Japanese occupation, but also 'the union of diverse nationalist groups under Communist direction'.

Nearing the end of the war in 1945, Japanese troops overthrew the French, before surrendering to the US and Chinese armies converging on Hanoi. Japanese policies led to a horrific famine, causing the deaths of two million North Vietnamese. Taking advantage of the unfolding chaos, the Viet Minh – funded, ironically, by the US Office of Strategic Services (OSS – the CIA's predecessor) – gained ground politically and territorially. Ho formed the National Liberation Committee and called for an uprising, the August Revolution, after which the north and the rest of Vietnam came under Viet Minh control. On 2 September 1945, Ho established the Democratic Republic of Vietnam with his Declaration of Independence Speech in Ba Dinh Square, near where he would later lie in state. This date became Vietnam's National Day and was also to be the date of Ho's death. As he read out his speech – modelled on the American Declaration of Independence – Ho was flanked by US OSS agents.

France's Last Stand

With the Chinese and French forces keen to re-impose colonial rule in his backyard, Ho took the lesser of the two evils, (reputedly remarking, 'I prefer to smell French shit for five years, rather than Chinese shit for the rest of my life'), in negotiating Vietnam's future. Relations with France deteriorated rapidly and the Franco-Viet Minh War broke out in December 1946. With President Ho's call for a general offensive, thousands took up arms.

The Old Quarter – known as 'Inter Zone I' and under Vietnamese control – experienced fierce resistance and street battles against the French in the first few months. In the face of a superior firepower (bankrolled by the US), Viet Minh troops retreated to the countryside. Funded by the new People's Republic of China, the Viet Minh adopted Mao Zedong's guerilla tactics, attacking and sabotaging isolated French units. This strategy was put to great effect at Dien Bien Phu (west of Hanoi) in 1954, where French troops surrendered to Viet Minh forces led by General Giap (an ex-professor at Hanoi University), thus ending the war and French colonial rule. Author Graham Greene, in Hanoi as a war correspondent, noted that Dien Bien Phu, 'marked virtually the end of any hope the Western powers might have entertained that they could dominate the East'. The Geneva Accord temporarily divided the

Above: General Giap planning the war against French forces
Right: South Vietnam's ARVN forces in a reconnaissance mission

country at the 17th Parallel: the north, the Democratic Republic of Vietnam (Communist under Ho); the south, the Republic of South Vietnam (non-Communist, under Catholic President Ngo Dinh Diem).

The American Factor

In gaining independence and French withdrawal, Vietnam lost its unity. The stipulated elections never occurred and the two polarised Vietnams had no diplomatic, cultural or commercial relations until 1975. Hanoi's National Liberation Front (NLF) aimed for reunification and instigated revolutionary, armed activities against the unstable southern regime. The southern Communist movement – Viet Cong (VC) – grew in momentum in the early 1960s and North Vietnamese Army (NVA) units, weapons and supplies were sent south, via the Ho Chi Minh Trail, to aid the VC.

The 'American War' stemmed from paranoia about Communism in the US: America believing that if South Vietnam fell under Communist control, other Southeast Asian nations would follow – the 'domino effect'. Economic aid and military advisers sent to the Republic of South Vietnam grew into a US military protectorate, then full-scale war in 1965 between US troops – siding with the Army of the Republic of South Vietnam (ARVN) – and the NVA and VC. Communist guerilla tactics redefined the nature and history of warfare. North Vietnamese resilience – based on a village-centred agricultural system – allowed it to carry on the war, despite a technologically superior opponent and prolonged, concentrated bombing campaigns: notably 'Operation Rolling Thunder' and the 'Christmas Bombing'. The latter saw 40,000 tons of bombs dropped over Haiphong and Hanoi over 12 days in December 1972, causing widespread damage and civilian deaths.

The 1973 Paris Accord provided a cease-fire and a withdrawal of US troops: for the first time in almost a century, no foreign forces occupied North Vietnam. Yet again, the price of war was horrendous: about one million North Vietnamese and VC troops were killed, as well as two million Vietnamese civilians (many in the north from US bombings). Ho Chi Minh died in 1969 without seeing his vision of a unified Vietnam become a reality.

Reunification and Doi Moi

War continued between the north and south. In 1975, Communist forces moved south, the ARVN crumbled and Saigon (renamed Ho Chi Minh City) surrendered to the North Vietnamese on 30 April. Vietnam was finally reunified in 1976 under the Communist Party. But the Socialist Republic of Vietnam, led from Hanoi, was faced with repairing its devastated economy and infrastructure, while integrating two different socio-economic systems. Wars continued, including an 11-year occupation of Cambodia and China's brief invasion in retaliation. Diplomatically isolated, Vietnam's alliance with the Soviet Union wasn't a wise political move, though advantageous financially. Many North Vietnamese spent time in the Soviet Union; some Soviet-style influences – buildings and services – are a permanent legacy in Hanoi.

Vietnam shut itself off from the outside world and experienced a harsh regime – ironically, at the hands of its own people. Faced with famine in the north, economic blunders and, later, the Soviet Union's demise (along with its funding), the Communist Party had to 'change or die'. A socio-economic reform programme called *doi moi* ('renovation') was launched in 1986 and opened the door to foreign investment, trade and tourism. Relationships were renewed with old foes France, the US and China.

Hanoi Today

Ironically, this city of fiercely independent people possesses an unmistakable European style. Hanoi's faded elegance is part of its French legacy, although residents might be loathe to admit this. The Gallic influence stems not only from colonial embellishments, but in its café society, churches, food and flourishing arts scene. With its galleries, street cafés and leafy boulevards, some parts resemble Paris. Interspersed with Chinese-style pagodas and grim Soviet-style architecture, Hanoi is a fascinating city of contrasts.

The city's relatively intact ancient and colonial quarters and limited modern development is not due to conservation; rather, a lack of financial resources, wars and ideological isolation. However, behind the sleepy façade, innovative foreign and local chefs, designers and entrepreneurs are helping to turn Hanoi into a hotspot of global cosmopolitanism.

You can't blame Hanoians for their wariness of foreigners – even though the recent 'invasion' is friendly. And there's a definite case for Hanoian arrogance – but you'd be too, if you had kicked out the US, Japanese, Chinese, French, McDonalds *and* displaced Pol Pot's Khmer Rouge regime. It has been

a long, tragic journey to peace and stability. Hanoians are now entangled in rapidly changing times, caught in a twilight zone of old Socialist policies and bureaucracy, mixed with a developing market economy and Western culture. Somewhat dour and reserved, Hanoians may greet you with blank stares. Smile back, however, and you will be rewarded with the most disarming of smiles.

Left: the modern face of Hanoi

history/culture

HISTORY HIGHLIGHTS

696–258BC Van Lang Kingdom ruled by Hung Kings; era of Dong Son culture.

257BC Thuc Lan establishes the Au Lac Kingdom.

207BC Chinese General Trieu Da conquers Au Lac, becomes part of the independent north Nam Viet Kingdom.

111BC Han Chinese Emperors annexe Nam Viet; start of Chinese rule in north.

AD40–43 Trung sisters organise rebellion against the Chinese.

938 Ngo Quyen defeats the Chinese at Bach Dang River.

1010–1225 Ly Thai To founds Ly Dynasty and Dai Viet; Buddhism flourishes; capital named Thang Long (Hanoi).

1288 General Tran Hung Dao defeats Mongolian forces at Bach Dang.

1428–1788 Le Loi, who assumes the name Le Thai To, ends 20-year Chinese occupation and founds Le Dynasty.

1592–1788 Country ruled by Trinh lords (north), Nguyen lords (south), divided into two in 1674. French missionaries become active. In 1627, Alexander de Rhodes adapts the Vietnamese language to a Romanised version.

1802 Nguyen Phuc Anh defeats Tay Son brothers, proclaims himself Emperor Gia Long of Nguyen Dynasty, unites present-day Vietnam and moves capital to Hué. Donh Kinh becomes regional capital and is renamed Hanoi.

1859 French forces capture Saigon.

1867 Cochin China (south) becomes French colony.

1883 Hanoi under French control. Annam (Central) and Tonkin (North) become French protectorates, which together with Cochinchina becomes the Indochina Union in 1887.

1890 Birth of Ho Chi Minh.

1902 Hanoi becomes the capital of French Indochina.

1911 Ho leaves Vietnam for 30 years.

1930 Ho founds the Indochinese Communist Party.

1940 Japanese forces occupy Indochina.

1941 Ho returns to Vietnam; founds the Viet Minh.

1945 Japan surrenders and the last Nguyen emperor abdicates. August Revolution leads to Viet Minh control and Democratic Republic of Vietnam.

1946 Hostilities lead to the Franco-Viet Minh War.

1954 Viet Minh victory at Dien Bien Phu ends war. Geneva Accord divides Vietnam: North is Communist under President Ho Chi Minh; South is non-Communist under President Diem. French troops withdraw.

1960 Hanoi forms National Liberation Front, uniting armed Communist forces in south – called Viet Cong (VC).

1962 12,000 US military 'advisers' move into the south.

1963 President Diem assassinated in a coup.

1965 Arrival of US combat troops; targets are bombed in the north.

1968 VC launches southern Tet Offensive; Mai Lai massacre.

1969 Ho Chi Minh dies; US commences phased troop withdrawal.

1972 US bombing campaign in north.

1973 Paris Accord cease-fire and US troops withdrawal.

1975 South surrenders to North Vietnamese Army; fall of Saigon which is renamed Ho Chi Minh City.

1976 Socialist Republic of Vietnam under Communist Party reunifies Vietnam.

1977 'Boat people' flee economic blunders and repression.

1978–89 Vietnam invades Cambodia.

1979 China invades North Vietnam.

1986 *Doi moi* ('renovation') reforms.

1993 US allows release of IMF loans to Vietnam.

1994 US lifts 30-year trade embargo.

1995 Diplomatic ties with US restored; US embassy opens in Hanoi. Vietnam becomes ASEAN member.

1997 Asian economic crisis; foreign companies take flight.

2001 US bilateral trade agreement.

2003 Vietnam hosts 22nd SEA Games.

2004 Vietnam's economy shows some significant signs of recovery.

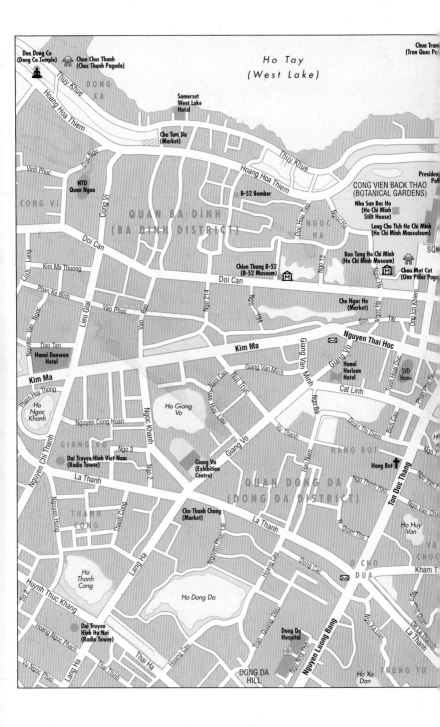

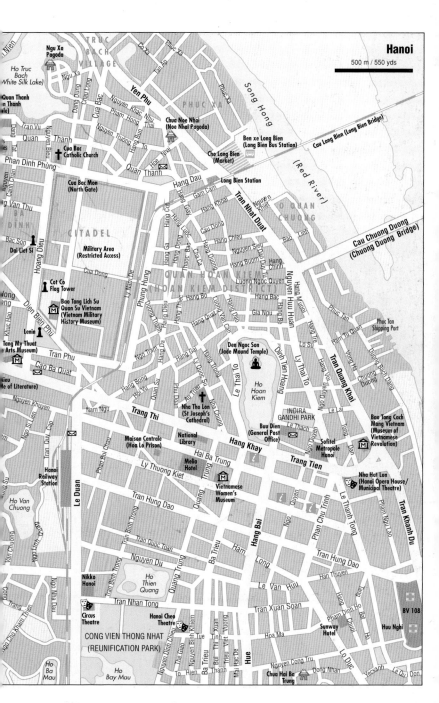

Hanoi

500 m / 550 yds

Truc Bach Village
Ngu Xa Pagoda
Ho Truc Bach (White Silk Lake)
Ngu Xa
Co Xa
Phuc Xa
Tan Ap
Yen Phu
Phuc Xa
Quan Thanh Temple
Dang Dung
Chau Long
Cua Bac
Nguyen Khac Nhu
Pham Hong Thai
Song Hong
Tran Vu
Quan Thanh
Cua Bac Catholic Church
Nguyen Truong To
Hoe Nhai
Chua Noe Nhai (Noe Nhai Pagoda)
Ben xe Long Bien (Long Bien Bus Station)
Cau Long Bien (Long Bien Bridge)
Phan Dinh Phung
Quan Thanh
Cho Long Bien (Market)
(Red River)
Cua Bac Mon (North Gate)
Hang Dau
Long Bien Station
Ga Long Bien
Tran Nhat Duat
Nguyen Thiep
O QUAN CHUONG
Bac Son
Dai Liet Si
Hoang Dieu
CITADEL
Military Area (Restricted Access)
Gam Cam
Hang Giay
Hang Khoai
Cau Dong
Hang Chieu
Bao Linh
Cau Chuong Duong (Chuong Duong Bridge)
Cot Co Flag Tower
Cua Dong
Hang Ga
Hang Dong
Thuoc Bac
Cha Ca
Nguyen Sieu
Hang Buom
Hang Chinh
Dien Bien Phu
Bao Tang Lich Su Quan Su Vietnam (Vietnam Military History Museum)
Ly Nam De
QUAN HOAN KIEM (HOAN KIEM DISTRICT)
Luong Ngoc Quyen
Nguyen Huu Huan
Hang Muoi
Phuc Tan
Phuc Tan Shipping Port
Lenin
Tang My Thuat (Fine Arts Museum)
Tran Phu
Cao Ba Quat
Hang Bong
Phung Hung
Duong Thanh
Hang Dieu
Hang Thiec
Hang Thiec
Hang Bo
Hang Can
Hang Bac
Gia Ngu
Lo Su
Phuc Tan
Tran Quang Khai
Duong Bach Dang
Chuong Duong
(Temple of Literature)
Nam Ngu
Hang Gai
Hang Da
Luong Van Can
Hang Trong
Den Ngoc Son (Jade Mound Temple)
Le Thai To
Dinh Tien Hoang
Ly Thai To
Nguyen Khuyen
Ngo Si Lien
Tran Quy Cap
Trang Thi
Ly Quoc Su
Nha Chung
Au Trieu
Nha Tho Lon (St Joseph's Cathedral)
Ho Hoan Kiem
INDIRA GANDHI PARK
Le Thach
Bao Tang Cach Mang Vietnam (Museum of Vietnamese Revolution)
Hanoi Railway Station
Ho Van Chuong
Maison Centrale (Hoa Lo Prison)
National Library
Phu Doan
Quang Trung
Hai Ba Trung
Hang Khay
Buu Dien (General Post Office)
Le Lai
Sofitel Metropole Hanoi
Le Duan
Ly Thuong Kiet
Melia Hotel
Trang Tien
Nha Hat Lon (Hanoi Opera House/ Municipal Theatre)
Tran Hung Dao
Vietnamese Women's Museum
Ba Trieu
Ham Long
Hang Bai
Ngo
Phan Chu Trinh
Le Thanh Tong
Pham Ngu Lao
Tran Khanh Du
Tran Binh Trong
Tran Quoc Toan
Nikko Hanoi
Nguyen Du
Ho Thien Quang
Tran Nhan Tong
Quang Trung
Le Van Huu
Tran Hung Dao
Han Thuyen
Circus Theatre
Hanoi Cheo Theatre
Nguyen Dinh Chieu
The Giao
Nguyen Binh Khiem
Tran Xuan Soan
Pham Dinh Ho
Lo Duc
Sunway Hotel
BV 108
Huu Nghi
CONG VIEN THONG NHAT (REUNIFICATION PARK)
Ho Ba Mau
Ho Bay Mau
Nguyen Dinh Chieu
Tran Binh
Ba Trieu
Bui Thi Xuan
Trieu Viet Vuong
Mai Hac De
Hue
Nguyen Cong Tru
Dong Nhan
Chua Hai Ba Trung
Vercanh
Le Dai Don

City Itineraries

The political and cultural capital of Vietnam, Hanoi is one of Asia's loveliest cities, with parks, lakes, tree-lined boulevards and history-drenched architecture. Hanoi's development may lag behind other Asian capitals, but this is good news for most visitors. The city still retains its unique identity, with a collection of legend-strewn lakes, low-rise colonial buildings and ancient pagodas – rather than glittering skyscrapers and shopping malls – dominating the city centre.

The city centre, which contains Hanoi's main areas of interest, is relatively small, with a distinct provincial feel. This makes travelling around the city relatively easy (*see pages 92–93*). There are many interesting must-sees, but Hanoi's main draw is its ambience and street life, a drama that unfolds daily on the streets, and in temples and markets. The best way to appreciate this mesmerising city is on foot. Take your time to savour its captivating sights, absorbing the sounds and aromas found at every corner you take, but watch yourself with the anarchic motorbike traffic, which needs constant attention (especially when crossing the road and skirting around congested pavements). When you tire, there is always transport on hand in the form of cyclos (three-wheeled pedicabs) and taxis. While some walks can be draining and exasperating you will be amply rewarded by one of Asia's most historic and atmospheric cities.

Itineraries 1–3 take in the highlights of the three main areas of interest in three full-day tours: the Old Quarter just north of Hanoi's central feature, Hoan Kiem Lake; the charming French Quarter; and the diplomatic area in Ba Dinh District. Itineraries 4–9 dip into further pockets of interest in and around the city, with morning and afternoon options. Hanoi is also the gateway to the Red River Delta – with its sacred pagodas and artisan villages – and the north, with its stunning mountain scenery and diverse ethnic minority groups. Along with breathtaking Halong Bay, Excursions 1–6 capture these sights and more, offering one to a few days away from the city.

Travel Essentials

Hanoi's summer months can get very hot with high humidity, making sightseeing hard work. With this in mind, set off early to avoid the heat and to fit everything in – the Vietnamese start their day very early and drop everything for lunch, usually 11.30am–1.30pm. Most attractions and services close at lunch time and many museums close on Mondays and Fridays. When visiting pagodas and temples, wear modest attire.

Left: a typical market scene in Hanoi
Right: a wizened local character

1. HOAN KIEM LAKE AND THE OLD QUARTER
(see map, p26)

This full-day walking tour gives a fascinating insight into the heart and soul of Hanoi. A stroll around legend-strewn Hoan Kiem Lake leads to the Old Quarter – a National Heritage Site loaded with sights. The day ends with a water puppet show, a unique northern art form.

The best way to appreciate this area is on foot as there is plenty to see and experience – but pay attention to the traffic. If you tire, hail a taxi or cyclo and regroup another time. Aim for an 8–8.30am start; breakfast is taken en route. Your starting point is the north end of Le Thai To Street, at the northwest tip of the Lake of the Restored Sword (Ho Hoan Kiem) – commonly known as Hoan Kiem Lake. Early on your route you will pass the Water Puppet Theatre where tickets can be purchased for an evening performance.

Hoan Kiem Lake is steeped in legend. In the 15th century, Emperor Le Thai To was supposedly handed a magic sword by a divine tortoise living in the lake, helping him repel Chinese invaders. After the country had been liberated, the tortoise snatched back the sword and disappeared into the lake – hence the name. Eight species of tortoises currently live in the lake. Hoan Kiem was once part of the Red River and a deep swamp, the surrounding area comprising marshland and small lakes, ringed with stilt houses and dotted with small islands, until the French drained the land in the 19th century.

The symbolic centre of modern Hanoi, Hoan Kiem is particularly lively at dawn, when locals get together for *t'ai chi*, aerobics and badminton, serenaded by booming music.

Above: Rising Sun Bridge (The Huc) leading to Ngoc Son Temple. **Right:** the legendary tortoise of Hoan Kiem Lake

Around Hoan Kiem Lake

Heading south down **Le Thai To Street**, to your right is a **statue of Emperor Le Thai To** (the street's namesake) and to your left, on an islet in the lake, the three-tiered, 18th-century **Tortoise Tower** (Thap Rua) dedicated to the mythical creature. At the southern end of Ly Thai To Street, stop for breakfast at the **Highlands Coffee** lakeside café.

Continuing on your walk, a small tower called **Hoa Phuong** – opposite the General Post Office – marks the entrance to the **former Bao An Pagoda** complex, which was destroyed by the French in the 1890s to make way for their new city. The park on your right – popular with the French for its outdoor concerts – was renamed **Indira Gandhi Park** in 1984, following the assassination of India's Prime Minister – a huge supporter of Vietnam. A massive bronze statue of Ly Thai To (founder and first king of the Ly Dynasty), recently unveiled here, dominates the park.

The austere, Soviet-style **Hanoi People's Committee Building** (to the right) stands in sharp contrast to the delicately arched, red-lacquered wooden **Rising Sun Bridge** (The Huc), leading to the **Ngoc Son Temple** (Den Ngoc Son), also known as the 'Temple of the Jade Mound' (daily 8am–6pm; admission charge). The temple is mainly associated with Tran Hung Dao, the general who defeated the Mongols at the Bach Dang River in 1279.

Note the temple's **Writing Brush Tower** obelisk on the left, inscribed with 'a pen to write on the blue sky' in three large Chinese characters. The temple was part of a 15th-century complex of palaces, pagodas and temples, dedicated to national heroes. What remains today are mostly 19th-century buildings, one displaying a giant tortoise that lived in the lake. The souvenir art shop opposite was formerly part of the temple complex but is now permanently separated by a road.

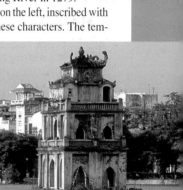

Next, pop into the nearby **Thang Long Water Puppet Theatre** (Mua Roi Nuoc Vietnam) at 57 Dinh Tien Hoang Street for tickets for tonight's hour-long performance (daily 5.15pm, 6.30pm, 8pm; admission charge; tel: 04-825 5450).

Walk up **Ho Hoan Kiem Street**, leading to Cau Go Street: across the road, flower stalls mark the start of **Hang Be Market**. Walk through the market, turn left and exit on **Dinh Liet Street** – the start of Hanoi's most famous sight, the Old Quarter.

Hanoi's Old Quarter

The **Old Quarter** (Pho Phuong) is an ancient merchants' quarter which evolved in the 13th century when 36 artisan's guilds concentrated around the Citadel to serve the court. This area was enclosed behind massive ramparts and heavy, wooden gates. The guilds developed independently, separated from each other by large walls and gates, locked at night.

Each of the 36 streets was named according to the merchandise on offer;

Right: Tortoise Tower on Hoan Kiem Lake

for example, *Hang* (merchandise) *Buom* (sails). Today, many streets have changed their wares, but some still specialise in the original craft. Each guild had a pagoda (*chua*), temple (*den*) and communal house (*dinh*).

The Old Quarter still retains many 'tube houses', so-called because of their narrow façades and long length. These single-storey shops belie their depth, containing dwellings at the rear and tiny courtyards. Feudal laws taxed shops according to their width – explaining why many are less than 3 m (10ft) wide – and decreed buildings should be no higher than a passing royal palanquin, in deference to the emperor.

Over the years, many buildings incorporated Western influences, like balconies and additional floors. Despite changes imposed by the French and the advent of traffic, these streets still yield a tangible microcosm of Hanoi street life. Every step is an assault on the senses: hawkers carrying goods on bamboo shoulder poles, food stalls, artisan workshops and family life spilling out on to the pavements, as well as a blend of historical, residential and religious buildings.

Exploring the Old Quarter's Streets

Hang Bac is one of Hanoi's oldest streets. *Bac* means silver and silversmiths originally settled here casting silver bars and coins. Today, shops still sell silver. This area was one of the main resistance centres against the French colonialists. At the intersection with Ta Hien Street, the **Golden Bell Theatre** (Nha Hat Chuong Vang) – a traditional Vietnamese theatre – was once the Hanoi Guards' HQ. Freedom fighters stood on the theatre steps in 1947, pledging their allegiance to the cause. **No 47** is a well-preserved century-old house.

At the end of Hang Bac, gravestone workshops spill out onto the pavements. Head into **Ma May** (Rattan Street). Members of the notorious Chinese Black Flag Army – peasant mercenaries from Southern China – once lived here. In the 19th century, they helped the Vietnamese fight wars against various clans and the French. Many houses still have removable wooden fronts.

The Old Quarter's most noteworthy antique house is at **No 87**. This former Communal House (Gioi Thieu Nha Co So) – beautifully restored to its late 19th-century condition – is open to the public (daily 8am–5pm; admis-

sion charge). Another restored house, **No 69** – now transformed into the **69 Restaurant-Bar** – still bears a secret tunnel, used by resistance fighters, running through its walls. Don't miss **Huong Tuong Temple** (Den Huong Tuong) at No 64 – founded in 1450 (daily 9–11am, 3–7pm; free).

Above: gravestone carving in Hang Bac
Left: interior detail, White Horse Temple

Originally, a tributary ran parallel to **Hang Buom** (Sails Street), enabling boats to sail up here to buy nautical supplies. When the French filled in the To Lich River, merchants switched to selling imported goods and dried foodstuffs, still sold today. Many Chinese merchants settled here in the 17th century and this soon became Hanoi's most affluent area, as the Chinese monopolised local commerce. The community's communal House at **No 22** bears intricate rooftop ceramics.

White Horse Temple (Den Bach Ma) at No 76 Hang Buom Street, is the Old Quarter's most revered and ancient place of worship; its architecture influenced by the Chinese community (daily 7.30–11am, 1.30–6pm). Founded in 1010 and restored many times, this stunning temple honours the white horse that appeared to King Ly Thai To in a dream. For several decades this National Heritage Site doubled as a storage house and printing workshop. During the fight for independence from French rule, many resistance fighters hid in the temple.

Turn right into **Hang Giay** (Paper Street) – with dilapidated buildings crammed with goods – and into **Nguyen Sieu Street**. Hanoi's first inhabitants settled along the banks of the To Lich River, which flowed where this street now runs. **Co Luong Temple** (Den Co Luong) is at No 28, its entrance flanked by two colourful guards.

Now pass along **Dao Duy Tu Street**, with its row of old houses, to reach **Old East Gate** (Cua O Quan Chong) – the only city gate to remain from the original 16 that once marked the city's entry points. To your left is **Thanh Ha Street**, a fascinating alley lined with market and food stalls. Follow it round, until you reach **Hang Chieu** (Mat Street), then **Hang Ma** (Paper Votive Street) – a mass of red, with lanterns and paper votive offerings used for Buddhist ceremonies.

Lunch Stop

For lunch, turn left into **Cha Ca Street** and head for No 14 – **Cha Ca La Vong** – a Hanoi institution (tel: 04-825 3929). This no-frills restaurant serves only a traditional Hanoi speciality, *cha ca* (grilled fish) – cooked at the table on a clay brazier – with noodles, herbs and peanuts. Listed under journalist Patricia Schultz's *1000 Places to See Before you Die*, this is allegedly the oldest restaurant in Vietnam (opened 1871).

Walk up Cha Ca Street, turn right into Hang Ca and right again into **Hang Duong** (Sugar Street). **Eastern Gate Pagoda** (Chua Cau Dong) at No 38b is an elaborately decorated pagoda, nearly 1,000 years old, with valuable statues and steles dating back 400 years. Further down, **Hang Ngang** (Crossways Street) was home to the Cantonese community. **Ho Chi**

Right: the Old East Gate entrance to the Old Quarter

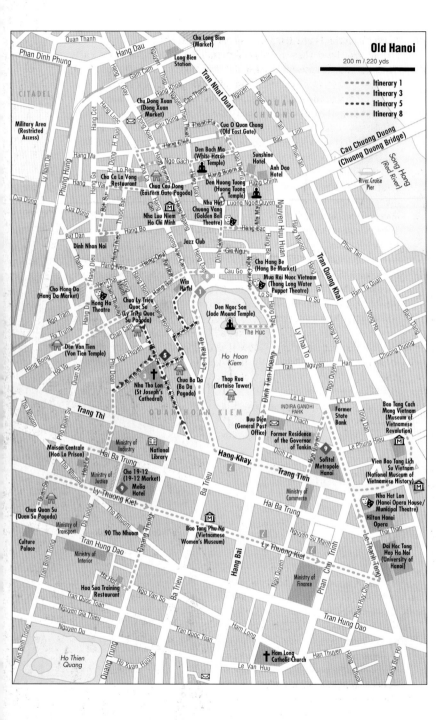

Old Hanoi

200 m / 220 yds

- Itinerary 1
- Itinerary 3
- Itinerary 5
- Itinerary 8

city itineraries

Minh Memorial House (Nha Luu Niem Ho Chi Minh) at No 48 was where Ho Chi Minh lived when he drafted Vietnam's Declaration of Independence; the house is now a museum (Mon–Sat 8–11am, 2–5pm, free, tel: 04-825 2622).

Retrace your steps, turning left into **Lan Ong Street**, where aromatic smells waft from stores selling roots, herbs and seeds used for traditional Chinese medicines. The street – named after an 18th-century physician and mandarin – once was home to a strong Chinese community – their communal house is at **No 42**. The traditional medicine shops continue into **Hang Vai** (Cloth Street), which specialises in bamboo.

Continue down **Bat Su** (China Bowls Street) as far as the intersection with **Bat Dan** (Wooden Bowls Street). To your right are some great noodle soup (*pho*) kitchens and opposite, at 33 Bat Dan Street, **Nhan Noi Communal House** (Dinh Nhan Noi). Head left along Bat Dan Street, turning into **Hang Thiec** (Tinsmith Street), a noisy workshop selling sheet metal goods. This western part of the Old Quarter was a revolutionary hotbed for the Vietnamese Patriotic Movement. December 1946 to February 1947 saw intense Old Quarter resistance against the French and Hang Thiec Street was a fierce battleground.

Turn left into **Hang Non** (Conical Hat Street). On the corner of **Hang Manh** (Curtain Street) several shops make and sell traditional musical instruments. **No 1** Hang Manh, a former barbershop, was used as a secret liaison office for the Hanoi Communist Party in 1938 and is now one of the city's best *bun cha* (barbecued pork patties with cold noodles) eateries (*see page 83*). **Hang Quat** (Fan Street) sells Buddhist and temple paraphernalia, ceremonial and festival items, plus wooden seals; look out for **Dau Temple** (Den Dau) at No 64. **To Tich Alley** – lined with food stalls and craft shops – leads to **Hang Gai** (Hemp Street), one of Hanoi's main tourist and shopping streets (*see page 51*).

Water Puppet Show

Depending on what time you have booked tickets for the Thang Long Water Puppet Theatre, there might be time before the performance for a spot of shopping or a drink in the Old Quarter area.

The art of water puppetry is unique to the Red River Delta – practised by rice farmers in flooded paddies for centuries. This delightful tradition, handed down the generations, nearly died out, but in the last 20 years or so a revival led to international tours and daily performances in Hanoi. Wooden puppets manipulated by bamboo sticks hidden beneath the water play out original stories based on folk tales and daily events, accompanied by traditional music.

Right: a water puppet show in Hanoi

2. BA DINH SQUARE, TEMPLE OF LITERATURE AND FINE ARTS MUSEUM *(see map, p29)*

A full-day tour which takes in the heart of Hanoi's political and diplomatic centre, including Ho Chi Minh's mausoleum, a temple dedicated to Confucius and a Fine Arts Museum. This is a tour for architecture lovers, with a contrasting blend of Chinese, Socialist and French styles.

The mausoleum closes Mondays and Fridays and for maintenance sometime during October and November. Weekends get very crowded with domestic visitors; dress respectfully, ie neatly, with no shorts or singlets. To get here, take a taxi to the Ho Chi Minh Mausoleum, passing the Vietnam Military History Museum along Dien Bien Phu Street at No 28 and the adjoining Cot Co Flag Tower (a remnant of the Citadel), which can be climbed. Aim to be at your starting point – 8 Hung Vuong Street, near Chua Mot Cot Street, at Ba Dinh Square – by 8.30am.

Ba Dinh Square

The difference between the Old Quarter's fascinating chaos and this area could not be more contrasting. Huge, austere **Ba Dinh Square**, with its Soviet-style architecture, is a sobering reminder of where you are – a Socialist Republic. This site of pilgrimage is where the former President of the Democratic Republic of Vietnam and founder of the Vietnamese Communist Party – Ho Chi Minh – lies for eternity in a massive, stark mausoleum (just like comrades Mao, Lenin and Stalin). In this very spot, Ho Chi Minh read out his Declaration of Independence on 2 September 1945: today, military parades and ceremonies occasionally take place here, watched by high-ranking party and government officials.

Ho Chi Minh Mausoleum

The **Ho Chi Minh Mausoleum** (Lang Chu Tich Ho Chi Minh) was built by the Soviet Union as a gift to the Vietnamese (Apr–Oct, Tue–Thu 7.30–10.30am, Sat–Sun, 7.30–11am; Nov–Mar, Tue–Thu 8–11am, Sat–Sun 8–11.30am; free). It was inaugurated on 29 August 1975 (although Ho Chi Minh died in 1969). The mausoleum has strict behavioural and dress codes and security measures. At the arrival point, leave your bags and personal effects in the designated cloakroom. Cameras, mobile phones, etc, are not allowed (keep your wallet/purse) and should be left behind here, or at nearby 'collection points'. Remember to collect your belongings before these close at 11am. Pass through

Above: cyclists riding past the Ho Chi Minh Mausoleum

security control and – under the intimidating gaze of soldier guards – queue in strict line. As you approach the mausoleum, it's prudent to stop talking or laughing, take your hands out of your pockets (and hats if you're wearing one) and adopt a respectful demeanour: if you forget, the guards will certainly remind you.

Inside a cold room, visitors slowly file past Ho Chi Minh's embalmed body lying in a glass casket. In the past, when the mausoleum closed for 'maintenance' the body used to be packed off to Russia for reembalming; apparently this is now undertaken in Hanoi. It's ironic that the egalitarian, unassuming Ho lies in a huge memorial: his last wish was to be cremated. However, given the reverence to the 'forefather of modern Vietnam' this wasn't a feasible option. Foreigners may find this whole process laughable, but to the Vietnamese, paying due respects to 'Uncle Ho' is an almost sacred task.

Presidential Palace and Ho Chi Minh's Stilt House

Exit the other side, where you are ushered to the next part of the grounds, **Ho Chi Minh's Relic Area** (Tue–Thu, Sat–Sun 7.30–11.30am, 2–4pm; addmission charge). Through wooded gardens, pass the magnificent **Presidential Palace**. Unless you have an invite, this is the nearest you'll get, as the restored colonial building is closed to the public. Built in 1906, this was home to several governor-generals of Indochina and is now used by the President. For the last 15 years of his life, Ho used the Presidential Palace for government council and receiving guests, but because of his simple lifestyle, he refused to reside here.

Instead, Ho lived in two unassuming houses on the grounds: the first, **House No 54**, is on your left (access isn't possible, but peeks through the windows are), and the other, a specially constructed stilt house further to your right, beside a picturesque carp pond.

Ho Chi Minh's Stilt House (Nha San Bac Ho) was where Ho worked and lived from 1958–69. Beautifully preserved with varnished wood and split bamboo screens, the modestly furnished quarters consist

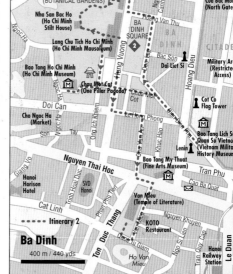

Above: interior, Ho Chi Minh's Stilt House

of an upstairs study and bedroom, plus an open, ground-floor meeting room. It was in a rear building that Ho passed away on 2 September 1969.

Ho Chi Minh Museum and One Pillar Pagoda

The next stop is the **Ho Chi Minh Museum** (Bao Tang Ho Chi Minh), a massive angular, Soviet-style monstrosity (Tue–Thu, Sat–Sun, 8–11.30am, 2–4pm; admission charge, tel: 04-846 3752). Dominating the tiny One Pillar Pagoda (*see below*), the museum opened on 19 May 1990 (the 100th anniversary of his birth). It celebrates Ho's revolutionary life, especially his exile years, and the pivotal role he played in Vietnam's history, in the context of international Communist development. Exhibits include countless photos, documents and personal effects, such as his rubber sandals, walking stick and the disguise he used to flee Hong Kong. But the exhibition departs from tradition with a surprisingly modern, almost surreal touch. Bizarre symbolic installations feature giant artificial fruit on enormous, lopsided furniture, a brick volcano and a even a totem pole. Try figuring out the symbolism.

The **One Pillar Pagoda** (Chua Mot Cot) is one of Hanoi's most recognised symbols. The original 11th-century version was blown up by French troops in 1954. This wooden pagoda, rising out a lotus pond, is a newer, smaller version built in the late 1950s; the single concrete pillar it stands on gives the game away. The pagoda is meant to resemble a lotus blossom, a Buddhist symbol of purity.

The adjacent **Dien Huu Pagoda** (Chua Dien Huu) is a welcome relief from all the ideology (daily 6–11am, 2–6pm). A monk practises acupuncture in one of the two buildings housed in a small courtyard.

Above: One Pillar Pagoda (Chua Mot Cot)

After the mausoleum closes, security relaxes somewhat and it's easier to wander freely around Ba Dinh Square. Walk along **Chua Mot Cot Street**, towards the intersection with **Dien Bien Phu Street**. French architectural influence is never far away; a prime example is the impressive **Ministry of Foreign Affairs** building (looking slightly out of place). More fine examples of alpine-style colonial buildings – housing embassies and diplomatic residences – are located at the top of Dien Bien Phu Street.

Back on Ba Dinh Square, return to the Presidential Palace to get a better full-on view, albeit from behind iron railings. Other colonial villas frame the square's northern boundary. Back down the square, on your left, is the **National Assembly Hall** and beyond this, **Heroes Memorial**. You may catch the **Changing of the Guard** ceremony outside the Mausoleum entrance, which usually takes place on the hour.

Taxis (or cyclos) are available from where you first arrived. Hop into one and en route to your lunch stop, **KOTO** (tel: 04-747 0337), at 61 Van Mieu Street, you pass along Le Hong Phong and Chua Van An streets. Here you can glimpse more striking French architecture in what is the city's diplomatic heartland. Alternatively, this route takes around 15 minutes to walk. KOTO, a delightful café-restaurant serving eclectic, international fare, doubles as a hospitality training school for disadvantaged Hanoi youth.

Temple of Literature

The **Temple of Literature** (Van Mieu) lies opposite (daily 8am–5pm; admission charge). Take a leisurely stroll to the two-tiered entrance gate on **Quoc Tu Giam Street**. The temple was founded in 1070 as Vietnam's principal Confucian sanctuary and to honour Vietnamese scholars. In 1076, Vietnam's first university, the National Academy (Quoc Tu Giam) was established here to educate future mandarins in Confucian doctrine. Despite the capital moving to Hué in 1802, examinations continued until the early 20th century, before the French put a stop to them.

An oasis of calm and beauty, the ground plan is modelled on the birthplace of Confucius, with five interconnecting walled courtyards, complete with gateways and lotus ponds. In the third courtyard, 82 stone stelae, mounted on tortoises, are inscribed with the names of 1,307 laureates of state examinations held

Above: souvenir shop at Ho Chi Minh Museum; **Right:** altar, Temple of Literature

at the National Academy from 1442–1779. The fourth courtyard holds the main temple buildings – a red-lacquered **House of Ceremonies and Sanctuary**, dedicated to Confucius. The fifth, final courtyard once housed the National Academy buildings; unfortunately these were destroyed by French bombs in 1947 and replaced since with a new two-storey pavilion. Traditional music recitals are performed here, subject to demand (and a small contribution).

Vietnam Fine Arts Museum

The **Vietnam Fine Arts Museum** (Bao Tang My Thuat), a five-minute walk away, is north of Van Mieu, at 66 Nguyen Thai Hoc Street (Tue, Thu, Fri and Sun, 8.30am–5pm, Wed and Sat 8.30am–9pm; admission charge, tel: 04-823 3084). This impressive building was formerly a boarding school for the children of Indochinese officials. After recent renovations, the highly-regarded museum now houses around 14,000 artworks from the pre-historic to the present. Exhibits are displayed on three floors with three annexes.

Highlights include a multi-armed *bodhisattva* statue, Cham statues, intricate woodcarvings, 18th-century wooden Buddhist statues and some impressive folk art, including ancestral worship pictures on a handcrafted paper called *do*. Most of the displays concentrate on the development of Vietnamese art from the 20th century to the present through paintings and sculpture – silk and lacquer are given special emphasis.

Taxis are located outside the museum and KOTO or flag one down. For dining options *see page 80 – Eating Out*. The evening can be rounded off with a cultural performance at the **Opera House**, **Ly Club** or the **Hanoi Cheo Theatre** (*see page 86*).

Above and left: façade and Cham sculpture at the Vietnam Fine Arts Museum

3. THE FRENCH QUARTER *(see map, p26)*

Hire a cyclo for the day for a ramble through Hanoi's French Quarter – a legacy of the Indochina era – with its wide tree-lined boulevards and marvellous colonial architecture. En route, take in key sights, including museums, markets, pagodas and more.

Ask your hotel to arrange a cyclo. Start around 9am at the St Joseph's Cathedral on Pho Nha Tho or Nha Tho Street (Church Street); the official entrance is via the Diocese of Hanoi compound (North Vietnam's centre of Catholicism) at 40 Nha Chung Street, a block away. Ask your driver to drop you there, then wait for you in front of the cathedral. Through the compound gates, walk down and turn right, bringing you directly to the cathedral's side entrance. If the door is closed, ring the bell.

St Joseph's Cathedral

St Joseph's Cathedral (Nha Tho Lon) is the one of the French Quarter's oldest buildings and Hanoi's only Gothic structure (closed 1–2pm for lunch). It was built by the French on the site of ancient Bao Thien Pagoda – demolished to make way for the cathedral – and consecrated on Christmas night in 1886. Many visitors have remarked that the Catholic cathedral resembles a smaller version of Paris' Notre Dame. Inside are beautiful stained-glass windows and an altar decorated with gold leaf. Regular masses are usually packed and at Christmas and Easter, Vietnamese-style biblical scenes are mounted on the front façade.

Leaving this lovely area (*see also page 40 – Itinerary 5*), drive down Au Trieu Street into the **French Quarter** proper; an area running roughly to the south and east of Hoan Kiem Lake, distinguishable by its grid system of wide, tree-lined boulevards dotted with elegant villas. Once Hanoi became Indochina's capital in 1902, the French laid down the groundwork for a new European town – the central area you will pass through today. Streets such as Trang Tien and Ngo Quyen had to be drained from former swamps and marshlands.

Hoa Lo Prison

Continue to Hoa Lo Street and the **Hoa Lo Prison**, or Maison Centrale as it was known during the French colonial period (daily 8.30–11.30am, 1.30–4.30pm, admission charge, tel: 04-824 6358). Opened in 1896, this walled prison compound once occupied an entire block, the largest French prison in North Vietnam. Two-thirds were demolished in 1993, making way for an office and apartment complex.

A small section now remains, preserved as a museum. Hanoi's notorious prison was dubbed the 'Hanoi Hilton' by US POWs incarcerated here dur-

Right: worshippers leaving St Joseph's Cathedral

ing the American War. These included Douglas Pete Peterson, the first US ambassador to the Socialist Republic of Vietnam, and US senator John McCain, who bailed out into Truc Bach Lake (*see page 48*).

Two fascinating rooms (if you can stomach the blatant propaganda) document the capture, incarceration and subsequent release of American POWs through a collection of photographs, documents and attire. Most of the museum concentrates on the plight of countless Vietnamese patriots and revolutionaries imprisoned and tortured here under French rule, pre-1954. Many grim, authentic relics remain, including instruments of torture, fetters, death-row cells and the guillotine – the way many inmates met their tragic deaths.

Pagodas, Markets and Museums

Quan Su Pagoda (Chua Quan Su) a block south at 73 Quan Su Street, is one of Hanoi's most active pagodas (daily 6am–9.30pm). Known as the 'Ambassadors' Pagoda', it was founded in the 15th century to house visiting Buddhist envoys and ambassadors. The pagoda's compound is now the headquarters of the Vietnam Unified Buddhist Association, a centre of Buddhist learning and research, and houses Vietnam's largest Buddhist library. Several monks reside here in its grounds.

Turn right out of the pagoda and right again, into **Ly Thuong Kiet Street**

– a wide, leafy boulevard lined with many fine examples of French architecture. On your left is one of Hanoi's oldest, most fascinating markets – **19–12 Market** (Cho 19–12). Its two covered lanes of stalls running through to the next street are crammed with fresh and live produce, dry goods, food stalls, kitchenware and clothes.

The market also has had an interesting history; it was allegedly a battleground where Hanoians fought against French occupying troops on 19 December 1946. Many locals were killed in the process and the site was turned into a mass grave. Post-reunification, it became an open-air market known as 'Hell's Market', but the name was later changed to commemorate the historic date. Another version alleges that it was once the collection point for bodies during an epidemic.

Now take a break for lunch: take the first right into Quang Trung Street. At the first junction on your right stands the imposing villa at **90 Tho Nhuom Street**, where a high-ranking French official resided, unaware that in 1930 the first General Secretary of the Indochinese Communist Party lived, worked and held political meetings in his basement!

Turn right into Ha Hoi Street, until you reach the **Hoa Sua Training Restaurant** (tel: 04-942 4448) at No 28a. Set in a gorgeous renovated villa, this restaurant is part of a non-profit organisation running hospitality training for Hanoi's disadvantaged youth. The largely French menu is surprisingly good and there are a few Vietnamese options as well. Service though can be a little slack.

Continuing to 36 Ly Thuong Kiet Street, where the **Vietnamese Women's Museum** (Bao Tang Phu Na Vietnam) is located (Tue–Sun 8am–4pm, admission charge, tel: 04-825 9936). Well worth a visit even if you're from the wrong gender, the three-storey museum runs four exhibitions with a wide range of photos, documents and displays. Vietnam's 'mother' figures and its women's contribution to the development of modern Vietnam and the Women's Union – with traditional dress and crafts from minority groups – all feature.

Opera House Area

At the end of Ly Thuong Kiet Street, turn left into **Le Thanh Tong Street** and note the impressive 1920s' building at the corner, which houses the medical and science annexe of the **University of Hanoi** – the former University of Indochina.

Le Thanh Tong and its surrounding streets are full of colonial villas housing diplomatic residences and embassies, but the most magnificent structure is the **Opera House**, or Municipal Theatre (Nha Hat Lon), on the corner of Trang Tien Street. Built by the French (modelled on the neo-Baroque Paris Opera), it opened in 1911 to keep the colonials entertained (and remind

Top left: John McCain's flight suit at Hoa Lo Prison; **Left**: Quan Su Pagoda
Right: exterior of Hanoi's Opera House

them of home). On 19 August 1945, the Viet Minh declared an independent democratic republic from the theatre's balcony, unfurling their banners in the process. Bullet holes from hand-to-hand fighting are still visible in the Opera House's Hall of Mirrors.

Restored to its former grandeur and re-opened in 1997, the Opera House is stunning, with a sweeping marble staircase, crystal chandeliers and red and gold leaf decor. Unfortunately, there are no tours or access, unless you have tickets for a cultural performance (details posted outside). Adjacent is the luxury **Hilton Hanoi Opera Hotel**, with a pleasing façade that replicates the style of the nearby Opera House; the interior, however, is modern.

History and Revolution Museums

Turn right into Trang Tien Street to visit the **National Museum of Vietnamese History** or Vien Bao Tang Lich Su Vietnam (Tue–Sun 8–11.30am, 1.30–4.30pm; admission charge, tel: 04-825 3518). This stunning, renovated building – typifying a hybrid Indochinese architecture – houses one of the city's best museums, with easy-to-follow displays, surprisingly low propaganda content and excellent archaeological and historical relics. Displays include ancient Dong Son bronze drums, Neolithic grave relics and clothes and artefacts belonging to the Nguyen emperors. Relics located in the grounds include the oldest epitaph in Southeast Asia, written in Sanskrit.

The **Museum of Vietnamese Revolution** (Bao Tang Cach Mang Vietnam) is opposite, at 216 Tran Quang Khai Street (Tue–Sun 8–11.45am, 1.30–4.15pm; admission charge, tel: 04-825 4151). Although it has a confusing layout and is in need of renovation, this museum – housed in a former customs house –

Above: interior, National Museum of Vietnamese History
Left: peasant statue in the Museum of Vietnamese Revolution

has an excellent collection of photographs, artefacts and original documents recording Vietnam's fight for independence from foreign occupation and the development of Vietnam's Communist Party and Socialist Republic.

Passing the Opera House again, turn right into **Ly Thai To Street**: passing the **Art Deco State Bank** (now converted into private offices) on your right. A sharp left into **Ngo Quyen Street** brings you to the stunning **Government Guesthouse**, which like the Opera House, is even lovelier lit up at night. Formerly the Residence of the Governor of Tonkin, the guesthouse is now the official residence for visiting VIPs. If you look close enough, you will see that the wrought-iron railings bear traces of bullet holes.

High Tea at the Sofitel Metropole

Opposite is the century-old **Sofitel Metropole Hotel** (tel: 04-826 6919). Apart from being an impressive example of colonial architecture – with its classical white façade – the former Grand Hotel Metropole Palace is steeped in history. Restored to its colonial-era charm, this was once the elegant epicentre for colonial society and one of Southeast Asia's greatest hotels. Former guests have included Noel Coward, Somerset Maugham, Charlie Chaplin (who spent his honeymoon here after his secret wedding to Paulette Goddard), Graham Greene (on assignment with *Paris Match* and writing part of *The Quiet American*) and Jane Fonda – who made her infamous 'Hanoi Jane' broadcasts to US troops during the 1972 US bombing campaigns.

Let your cyclo go and enjoy high tea (or a Graham Greene Martini) at the hotel's legendary **Le Club Bar** or **Bamboo Bar**, or opt for early dinner at its excellent, fine-dining restaurants, **Le Beaulieu** for French or **Spices Garden** for Vietnamese *(see page 81)*.

From the hotel, hop into a cyclo passing by the illuminated Opera House, then along Trang Tien Street. The former high street of colonial days now has galleries and book stores housed in a mix of French and dreary Soviet-style buildings.

After 8.30pm, you can catch live jazz at the **Jazz Club by Quyen Van Minh** at 31 Luong Van Can Street (tel: 04-828 7890). This was the first jazz venue in Vietnam, founded by the well known god father of Vietnamese jazz, Quyen Van Minh. Along with an ensemble of musicians, Minh plays the saxophone most nights. He is regularly joined on stage by visiting international musicians.

Right: façade of the old-world Sofitel Metropole Hotel

4. WEST HANOI *(see map, below)*

This morning tour combines a fascinating mix of sights located in the west of Hanoi: the innovative Museum of Ethnology, an artist's stilt house, an American B-52 bomber and the serene Botanical Gardens, rounding off with a seafood lunch at West Lake.

Ask your hotel to call Duc's Stilt House (Nha San Duc), tel: 04-762 5452 or 0913 228 113, informing them you'll be arriving before lunch (see details on getting there below). Local seafood restaurants are a lunch option, or bring a picnic to enjoy in the Botanical Gardens (weather permitting). Transport is by taxi. Aim to be at the Vietnam Museum of Ethnology by 8.30am; it is located on Nguyen Van Huyen Road, Cau Giay District, a 20-minute ride west of central Hanoi.

Vietnam Museum of Ethnology

Officially opened in 1997 by French President Jacques Chirac and designed with the help of the Musée de l'Homme in Paris, the **Vietnam Museum of Ethnology** (Bao Tang Dan Toc Hoc Vietnam) is perhaps Vietnam's most progressive museum (Tue–Sun 8.30am–5.30pm; admission charge; tel: 04-756 2193). A trip here here is highly recommended.

As a centre for research and conservation, the museum serves to promote a greater understanding of Vietnam's 54 ethnic minority groups – mostly residing in the northern mountainous regions. If you haven't the time to visit these ethnic groups, the museum is the next best thing to understanding their diverse heritage, culture and lifestyles. But even if you have planned to see ethnic minorities, a visit to the museum will certainly enhance your trip.

The museum is clearly signed and presented – for a small fee, a guide is available. The open-plan, two-storey museum – designed in the form of an ancient Dong Son drum – presents permanent displays of objects and documents relating to the culture and lifestyle of Vietnam's ethnic minority communities. On the ground floor are temporary exhibitions. To date, the museum has gathered nearly 15,000 ethnic artefacts from across Vietnam – including musical instruments, masks, baskets and garments – which are superbly showcased, as well as maps, wall charts and photographs.

Dioramas depict scenes such as conical hat production, markets and various ritual ceremonies – illustrated by audio-visual tapes. There is even a reconstruction of a traditional Black Thai house. Check the board outside the main entrance for information about open-air exhibitions in the grounds at the rear of the museum, where you'll also find a permanent display of authentic, life-size minority dwellings plus a grave-house – each a mini-museum.

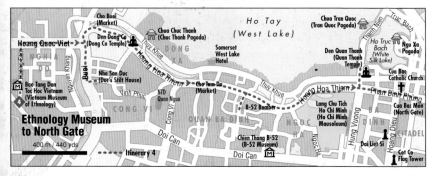

Your visit may coincide with occasional water puppet performances – these are more traditional than the ones staged elsewhere. There is also a very good museum shop with a decent map and book selection. Sales of crafts and souvenirs help ethnic communities earn income from their traditional skills.

Duc's Stilt House

The museum should give you a taste of what to expect at your next port of call – **Duc's Stilt House** or Nha San Duc (tel: 04-762 5452 or 0913 228 113). Take a taxi (or ask reception to call one) and head for Duong Buoi Street and Lane (Ngo) 462 – also known as Alley (Doc) K82, on your left. Head down here and turn first left. Just before No 16 on your right, there is a narrow alley: ask your driver to wait and walk down the alley. The stilt house is immediately on your left as you exit the alley.

Duc's relocated Muong ethnic minority stilt house is one of Hanoi's most active centres for installation exhibitions and performance art by contemporary artists. He is also a renowned ceramic collector and the upper floor studio is set aside for a veritable Pandora's box of antiquities as well as artefacts, purposely aged to look antique. Many items are for sale.

American War Relic

Driving back in the direction of town along **Hoang Hoa Thiem Street**, turn right into Lane 55 (Ngo 55), between No 55 and No 57; a blue sign marks the turning. Continue for 100m (328ft) until you reach the wreckage of an American **B-52 bomber**, semi-submerged in the middle of small **Huu Tiep Lake**, in Ngoc Ha village. This rusting undercarriage has laid here

Top: a minority communal house at the Vietnam Museum of Ethnology
Above: a half-sunken American B-52 bomber in Huu Tiep Lake

untouched since it was shot down on 27 December 1972 in the US-led 'Christmas Bombing' campaign during the American War. Residential houses, a school and café surround this permanent reminder of Vietnamese victory.

Botanical Gardens

Continuing in the same direction along Hoang Hoa Thiem Street, nearby, at No 3, are the gates of the **Botanical Gardens** (daily 7am–10pm). Leave your taxi here. The 100-year-old gardens are very picturesque, with two large lakes, mature trees, several varieties of plant species and sculptures – plus a children's play area, an aviary and a temple. This is one of the few gloriously peaceful spots in Hanoi and unlike Hoan Kiem Lake, you are left completely alone.

It's a perfect place for a picnic. However, if game for something more, walk along outside the garden railings heading east for about 10 minutes to the end of the street. This brings you to the southern end of **West Lake** (Ho Tay) and a small park. Along the water's edge running westwards is a narrow footpath, leading to a group of lakeside local seafood restaurants at **4 Thuy Khue Street**. After your hearty seafood dinner, flag down a taxi. Returning to the centre of town, ask the driver to go along **Phan Dinh Phung Street**, where you'll pass a few examples of French colonial architecture, **Cua Bac Catholic Church** and opposite, **North Gate** (Cua Bac Mon) – one of the few remnants of the 19th-century citadel. Cannonball damage, from the 1882 French siege, is still visible on its front walls.

5. NHA THO STREET SHOPPING *(see map, p26)*

Spend a morning soaking up the atmosphere on the streets surrounding St Joseph's Cathedral. Several innovative home decor, interior design, giftware shops and boutiques have burst on the scene: quality shopping is all found here, but cafés, galleries and ancient pagodas balance the retail therapy in this delightful area.

This tour can easily be done on foot: when you've had enough, cyclos, taxis and motorbike taxis are readily available in the area. Most shops open by 9am. Your starting point is in front of St Joseph's Cathedral (see page 33 – Itinerary 3) on Pho Nha Tho or Nha Tho Street (Church Street). Before you hit the streets, linger over breakfast at Moca Café (details below).

Moca Café (tel: 04-825 6334), on the corner of **Nha Tho Street** (Church Street) and in the shadow of **St Joseph's Cathedral**, is ideal for breakfast. A great place to watch the world go by, this European-style café roasts and grinds its own beans (hence the wafting aroma) and serves the best coffee in town. In winter months, the open fireplace is a cosy retreat from the chill.

Above: inside the Botanical Gardens
Right: upmarket silk and fashion shop in Hanoi's Old Quarter

After breakfast, follow **Au Trieu Street**, running along the cathedral's right-hand side. Down this quiet street are some funky stores, such as Japanese-run **Nagu** (No 10), which sells ceramics, and Australian-run **Things of Substance** (No 14), which has chic, off-the-rack separates and accessories. **Cherish Art House** (No 8) sells interesting contemporary and reproduction old photographs of Vietnam, as well as reproduction antiquities. **No 18** sells dozens of hand-made silk hair accessories, while **Lan Handicrafts** (No 28) – a non-profit organisation – sells handicrafts and quilts hand-made by young handicapped and disadvantaged Vietnamese. Along the street, pots of bubbling food and makeshift barbers hide under sweeping banyan branches.

Halfway down Au Trieu Street, on the left-hand side, an impressive entrance of ornate woodcarvings and a village gate herald **Que Gallery** (No 1) which sells traditional, countryside-themed Vietnamese art works, and, in an adjoining boutique, hand-made silk garments. On the trellis topped first-floor terrace, you can sip tea with the young artist-owner. Further down the street, on the right-hand side, **Seal Décor** (No 56) sells traditional, hand-made home furnishings and gifts, including reproduction antique Buddha busts and statues.

East meets West

Retrace your steps back to the cathedral, turning left into **Ly Quoc Su Street**. **Innove**, at No 15, sells stylish and quality hand-made lacquerware, infusing these Vietnamese products with contemporary designs. Walk past fruit stalls, a teashop and a makeshift barber to **No 25** where a faded yellow entrance gate adorned with Buddhist flags and blue dragon motifs leads to a small courtyard and the tiny **Phu Ung Temple** (Den Phu Ung). Built in 1830, it honours Vietnamese heroes General Tran Hung Dao and General Pham Ngu Lao, who fought invading Mongols.

Trinh Tuan and Cong Kim Hoa Art Studio (No 17) is the studio-home of two of Hanoi's leading lacquer artists, who also happen to be husband and wife – you are welcome to pop in. Refreshments are at hand at a popular local *bia hoi* (fresh beer outlet) on the corner of Chan Cam and Ly Quoc Su streets. Nearby, **Tuyet Lan** (No 10) – family-run since 1920 – specialises

in children's hand-made embroidered goods.

Returning to the cathedral, an ornate yellow and red gateway at No 50 marks the location of **Ly Trieu Quoc Su Pagoda** (Chua Ly Trieu Quoc Su). The stunning pagoda, built in 1131, has seen several overhauls but still remains beautifully preserved, noted for its richly carved decoration and spectacular collection of statues – some dating back to the 15th century. Your visit may coincide with daily prayers; remain at the back and soak in the mesmerising atmosphere.

Back at the square, with Nha Tho Street on your left, continue to **Nha Chung Street**. **L'image** (No 8 and No 34) has a lovely selection of quality, hand-made home decor and gifts, blending Oriental and Western designs and styles. Also at No 8, **Propaganda Art** sells Communist-style propaganda art posters – both original and reproduction – plus other kitschy artefacts.

If you're feeling peckish by now, the aptly named **No Noodles Sandwich Bar** (No 20) is the perfect lunch stop. It serves a variety of tasty baguette sandwiches and fruit juices.

After lunch, continue on your shopping jaunt. Italian-run **Oriental House** (No 28) has a particularly striking range of velvet and silk designs, while **Cocoon** (No 30) has a good reputation for tailoring and brightly coloured taffeta silk clothing with intricate embroidery.

Return to the square and turn right into Nha Tho Street, one of Hanoi's prettiest streets, and lined with old banyan trees. **Mosaique** (No 22) sells gorgeous hand-made fashions, home decor and lighting accessories – all combining Oriental flair and style with European contemporary practicalities,

and using quality local materials. At night, Mosaique illuminates the street with its display of coloured, multi-formed silk lanterns.

Long-established **Co** (No 18) is one of the more reliable tailors, specialising in linens and cottons. Italian-run **LaCasa** (No 12), a home decor and interior design company, takes traditional Vietnamese artisan techniques and products, adapting them to contemporary designs using local materials, such as mahogany and rosewood. **Red Door Deco** (No 15) retails authentic home furnishing antiques and finely crafted original, contemporary furniture. Next door, **Tina Sparkle** (No 17), an ultra-chic bags and accessories boutique, is a lighter, funkier version of its sister branch, **Ipa-Nima** (at 59G Hai Ba Trung); both selling flamboyant designer bags.

A French Ambience

If you need a further break from overt consumerism, enter the narrow gateway next to No 5 Nha Tho Street, for **Ba Da Pagoda** or Chua Ba Da (daily 8–11.30am, 1.30–9pm). The low-level façade belies the pagoda's depth and size and houses an impressive array of Buddha statues. Built in the 15th century, this is the second Buddhist Association headquarters in Hanoi.

Nha Tho Street smacks of French ambience: the faded yellow walls with green shutters, home to **Le Malraux** (No 6), could have come straight from a provincial French town. This Franco-Vietnamese café-bar sells original, French designed furniture.

Turn left into **Hang Trong Street**. On your left, **Viet Fine Arts Gallery** (No 96) is relatively new on the art scene. This spacious commercial gallery showcases Vietnamese art. Opposite, **Dome** (No 71b6–b7) is a joint-international store selling mostly innovative, high-quality giftware and home decor using Vietnamese materials. Centuries-old and miniscule **Dong Huong Communal House** (Dinh Dong Huong), at No 82, is somewhat hidden on the first floor, but worth a quick visit.

Café Society

Turn right into **Bao Khanh Street**: follow the street around, lined with bars and CD shops, until it merges into leafy **Hang Hanh** – originally 'Onion Street', now known as 'Café Street' for its local, street-side cafés. Go native: order a Vietnamese coffee (*ca phe phin*) and watch life on the street.

If you haven't had lunch, return to Nha Tho Street, where you'll find some excellent eating options. These include: **La Salsa** at No 25 (tel: 04-828 9052), a French-run Spanish tapas bar and restaurant; its neighbour **Mediterraneo** (tel: 04-826 6288), one of the best Italian restaurants in town; and the bistro-style **Paris Deli-Café** (tel: 04-928 6697). All have balconies overlooking the street.

Top left: accessories at LaCasa; **Left:** stylish shops along Nha Tho (Church) Street;
Right: worshipper offering joss sticks at Ba Da Pagoda

6. HANOI'S SUBURBAN VILLAGES *(see map, below)*

A morning tour to see Bat Trang ceramic village, the stilt house of a Vietnamese artist and lunch at Le Mat snake village.

Set off early: most tour companies include Bat Trang – 15km (9¼ miles) southeast of central Hanoi – in their itineraries. The trip can be done independently by car, taxi or motorbike. If you plan to visit Bat Trang only, it's a pleasant bicycle ride: alternatively, Red River Tourism (121 and 42 Chuong Street, tel: 04-826 1479) offers weekend boat cruises along the Red River to Bat Trang, stopping en route at temples and pagodas.

Across **Chuong Duong Bridge**, you'll get one of the best views of the expansive **Red River**. To your left are the rusted iron arches of **Long Bien Bridge**, now reserved only for trains, pedestrians and cyclists. The 1,682-m (5,581-ft) bridge was designed by the same team that constructed the Eiffel Tower. Opened in 1902, Long Bien Bridge was originally named after the then Governor-General of Indochina, Paul Doumer. Until Chuong Duong opened in 1985, this was the only bridge spanning the Red River. Of great strategic

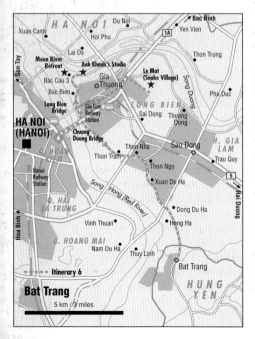

Above: cyclists crossing Long Bien Bridge

importance during the American War, Long Bien Bridge was bombed many times, but never taken out.

After Chuong Duong, turn first right, then continue along the Long Bien-Xuan Quan road. Part of this route comprises metropolitan Hanoi, but this dyke road – protecting the area from flooding – offers a predominately rural scene of villages and farming communities. The countryside around Hanoi is dotted with lush rice fields, market gardens, brick kilns, churches, temples and pagodas. But booming housing development – with soaring land prices – is changing the scenery forever. After about 11km (6¼ miles), an enormous sign heralds Bat Trang.

Bat Trang

Bat Trang ('the place where bowls are made') is actually an area consisting of two large villages, Giang Cao Village and Bat Trang Village. The 6,000 locals living here produce only one item, glazed ceramics. The first entrance leads into **Giang Cao Village**, a main drag lined with dozens of showrooms selling masses of ceramics and pottery: crockery, vases, bowls, tiles, ornaments, pots, huge urns for pagodas and household decorations. Many outlets in Hanoi sell products from Bat Trang but here, at the source, you have the widest choice and best prices. It's no surprise that this is the richest handicraft village in North Vietnam and the prosperity is quite evident.

Wandering down the alleyways, you'll find many family-based pottery workshops and kilns, where you are welcome to watch the whole process. Patterns are still painted by hand, and moulds and traditional brick kilns are used. However, a growing number of workers now use gas kilns these days. Although more expensive, gas is a far quicker and more reliable method and gives high-quality results. On walls across Bat Trang, the black blobs that you see hanging from walls and drying in the sun are in fact coal and mud cakes, used for kiln fuel.

Bat Trang was founded around the 14th century when brick craftsmen moved nearer to Hanoi for work. Quickly famed for their work, they were commissioned to supply bricks for the Citadel, but soon caught on that it was far more profitable (and easier) to produce ceramics instead. Being near to the river, white clay supplies and the easy access to the capital made the market extremely favourable. From 15th–18th centuries, Bat Trang was renowned for its ceramics both in Vietnam and overseas, selling to many Asian countries. When Chinese ceramics took over in popularity, Bat Trang produced solely for the domestic market. It was only post-1986 that Bat Trang's ceramics have seen a renaissance, with export sales booming once more.

Heading northeast, walk to the end of the main concrete drag, turn right and keep along the river until you reach **Bat Trang Village** proper, the oldest part of Bat Trang. With its high walled and narrow alleyways,

Right: pottery craftsman at Bat Trang

traditional production methods and lack of commercialism, this place is akin to a time warp and is in marked contrast to Giang Cao's bustling consumerism. A second entrance, about 1km (½ mile) from the first entrance, gives quicker and direct access to this village.

Anh Khanh's Studio

Retrace your way back to Hanoi; on nearing Chuong Duong Bridge, take the road that veers left under the bridge and then head along Gia Thuong dyke road, heading in the opposite direction from Bat Trang. After about 4km (2½ miles), on your right, you'll see a small sign, 'Studio Anh Khanh 100m', next to a larger sign announcing 'Gia Thuong village'. Take the slipway down the embankment, turn right, then first left into a wide alley to find **Anh Khanh's Studio** (tel: 04-827 1216/091 324 4354).

The studio is in fact an ethnic minority stilt house and Dao Anh Khanh's home, the ground floor littered with his contemporary oil paintings and sculpture. Anh Khanh, with his new genre of art, is one of Vietnam's most important and influential performance artists. A revolutionary visual artist who has gained considerable recognition overseas, he dabbles in sculpture and painting, but is mostly famous for performance art. If Anh Khanh is at home he will be quite happy to chat about his craft. Have a wander around the lush landscaped gardens surrounding his house, which is dotted with sculptures and installations, including a totem pole.

Retrace your route: passing under Long Bien Bridge, take a left turning into Ngoc Lam Street, which merges into Nguyen Van Cu Street. Across the other side of the roundabout, continue along Ngo Gia Tu Street (Highway 1a) until you see the sign for Le Mat village on your right.

Le Mat Snake Village

Visitors come to **Le Mat** ('Snake Village') purely to eat and drink snake delicacies – the streets are lined with snake restaurants. Groups of Vietnamese men are the main customers – snake meat and its various accompaniments are regarded as a natural aphrodisiac with medicinal properties. If you're feeling particularly brave, opt for the set menu that comprises 10–12 snake dishes: this includes snake in every conceivable form, plus snake's blood and bile mixed with rice wine, as well as the live beating heart (swallowed by males only). Restaurants usually offer this package at around US$10: recommended are **Quoc Trieu** (tel: 04-827 2988) and **Huong Que** (tel: 04-827 3323) restaurants. Choosing to view the killing and gutting of the chosen snake is optional.

Many restaurants house varieties of caged snakes on their ground floors. Many are bought or farmed, as it is now illegal to hunt snakes. Some snakes are extremely venomous, and the higher their medicinal quality, the higher the cost. You'll also see flagons of snake wine with snakes coiled up inside.

Above: gruesome snake killing at Le Mat village

7. WEST LAKE *(see map, below)*

This afternoon tour takes in the main sights around West Lake (Ho Tay), Hanoi's largest lake offering some of the city's most revered pagodas, a bronze-making village and other lakeside pursuits. A sunset drink affords fabulous views across the Red River before dinner.

This is mostly a walking tour, so be sure to wear suitable footwear, bearing in mind that you will be dining out later in the area. Taxis are used at the beginning and end of the tour. Ask your driver to take you first to Phu Tay Ho Temple on the northeastern shore of West Lake; tell him to wait at the large entrance gate at the end leading to the temple.

Phu Tay Ho Temple

Phu Tay Ho Temple (Den Phu Tay Ho) lies in a delightful courtyard setting on the shores of **West Lake** (daily summer 6am–9pm; winter 6am–7pm). This is one of the most popular places of worship in Hanoi: many locals flock here on Sundays and on the first and 15th day of each lunar month to pray for good fortune.

Dedicated to Thanh Mau (Mother Goddess) two lurid buildings in the temple complex are intricately adorned with numerous bat and dragon motifs and fairly heave with statues and temple paraphernalia. At the front of the

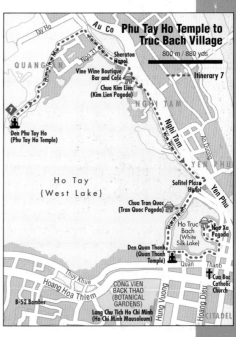

Above: Phu Tay Ho Temple

temple, large bronze urns under old banyan trees are used for burning offerings and incense.

Two Pagodas

Retrace your route by taxi, passing rambling lakeside stilt house restaurants serving local delicacies such as snails. Head for **Kim Lien Pagoda** (Chua Kim Lien), just off the Xuan Dieu and Yen Phu intersection (daily 6.30–11am and 1.30–5pm). Ask your driver to wait.

Kim Lien Pagoda is considered one of the most ancient and beautiful pagodas in Hanoi. Legend has it that it was built in the 12th century by Princess Tu Hoa, who later moved in and taught locals how to rear silk worms. Despite undergoing subsequent overhauls, the pagoda still retains its unique architectural style, with sweeping, curved roof lines and an unusual portico. Note the elaborately carved low wooden beams and numerous Buddhist statues. Nuns reside within the pagoda's compound.

Drive back down **Yen Phu Street**. In the 13th century, the Chinese established Yen Phu Village as an incense producing area, a craft still practised by some locals today.

The next stop is **Tran Quoc Pagoda** (Chua Tran Quoc) which lies on an islet on West Lake, off Thanh Nien Road (daily 7–11.30am, 1.30–6.30pm). Palm trees and a striking red brick stupa in the grounds mark the location. Let your taxi go at this point.

Founded in the 6th century, Tran Quoc Pagoda was relocated here in the 17th century from a site prone to flooding. Considered Hanoi's oldest pagoda and a magnificent symbol of Vietnamese Buddhism, this was formerly the Buddhist centre of ancient Hanoi. A stele from 1639 details its history.

West Lake's Attractions

Walk down **Thanh Nien Road**. **West Lake** (Ho Tay), roughly 13km (8 miles) in circumference, is another lake steeped in legend. Once ringed with magnificent palaces, it is now undergoing massive development, once more a sought-after place to reside. In 1619, villagers built this road dividing the lake into two parts: West Lake on your right and the smaller Ho Truc Bach – or **Truc Bach Lake** as it's commonly known – to your left.

This flame-tree lined causeway is delightful in summertime when locals flock here in droves to relax, have some ice cream and snacks and go boating (there are several boat hire kiosks).

A **memorial** further down on your left is dedicated to anti-aircraft gunners in the American War; former US pilot (later Senator) John McCain parachuted into Truc Bach Lake in 1967. A photograph of this is

Above: Kim Lien Pagoda; **Left:** Tran Quoc Pagoda; **Right:** West Lake at sunset

displayed in Hoa Lo Prison (*see page 33 – Itinerary 3*) where he spent some time as a POW.

Quan Thanh Temple (Den Quan Thanh) is at the end of Thanh Nien, adjacent to Truc Bach Lake (daily 8am–4pm; admission charge). Originally built in 1010, rebuilt in 1677 and restored in 1893 and 1998 – the Taoist temple houses a 4-ton (4,064-kg), 375-m (1,230-ft) tall black bronze statue of the genie Tran Vu, Guardian of the North (to whom this temple is dedicated). The temple is also known for its wooden boards carved with Chinese couplets known as 'parallel sentences' and horizontal boards carved with poems. The magnificent entrance contains a bronze bell almost 2m (6½ ft) in length, and like the statue, cast in 1677. On the first and fifteenth days of the lunar month, the temple is packed with worshippers, rubbing money on Tran Vu's foot for good luck.

Leave the temple, turn right into Thanh Nien Street and right again into **Tran Vu Street**. This takes you along Truc Bach Lake's south side. Truc Bach translates as 'White Silk'. An 18th-century summer palace used as a detention centre for wayward (or unwanted) concubines, condemned to weave fine white silk, once stood here.

Continue along Tran Vu – passing **Chau Long Market** (Cho Chau Long) and **Chau Long Pagoda** (Chua Chau Long). This pagoda, ringed by high walls and palm trees, is also used as a school for Buddhist monks.

Ngu Xa Bronze Casting Village

Cross the bridge over the canal, take the next right into **Nguyen Khac Hieu Street**: you are now in the bronze casting village of **Ngu Xa** (also known as Truc Bach). This is a traditional art form in Vietnam; in the 16th century, bronze-casters lived here, casting items (such as the statue in Quanh Thanh Temple) for pagodas and the Citadel. Although Ngu Xa is still renowned for bronze casting, but only a few households practise this craft today.

Ngu Xa was once a small island in the lake, but is now connected to the

mainland. Although there has been a lot of new housing development, it's still an interesting place to wander around. The village is also famed for its cock fighting events. Walk down Nguyen Khac Hieu Street: on your left, on the corner of Ngu Xa Street, is **Ngu Xa Pagoda** (Chua Ngu Xa; also known as Than Quang Pagoda), home to an enormous Amitabha Buddha statue – the largest monolithic bronze statue in Vietnam. This weighs 10 tons (10,160 kg) and, incredibly, was cast in a single day in 1952 with the help of the entire village! The pagoda had to be rebuilt to house the statue.

Exit the grounds, turn left into Nguyen Khac Hieu Street: **Nam Trang Communal House** (Dinh Nam Trang) is on your left. The 400-year old *dinh* has served many roles, including rice store and police station. Note the elaborate woodcarvings (some with real gold leaf) – typical of North Vietnam.

To see a bronze casting workshop, continue to the end of the street, turn left into Nam Trang Street. At No 15, turn right down an alleyway opposite, which leads to lakeside Tran Vu Street, then turn right. Continue until you reach No 178c: next door there is a workshop where you can watch bronze casting work in progress.

Red River Sunsets

Next stop is the luxury **Sofitel Plaza Hanoi Hotel**, just north of Truc Bach Lake, at 1 Thanh Nien (tel: 04-823 8888). To get there, either continue right around Truc Bach, but better still, retrace your steps back to Quan Thanh Temple and along the causeway leading to the Sofitel. Once there, head for a well-earned drink and the best views of the Red River and city – and if lucky, a fabulous sunset – from the 20th-floor Summit Lounge. Weather permitting, sunset barbecues are hosted on the bar's open terrace.

Alternatively, hail a hotel taxi and head to 1a Xuan Dieu Street and the excellent **Vine Wine Boutique Bar and Café** (tel: 04-719 8000), which serves fine international food and wines in exquisite surroundings. The wood-fired oven pizzas are excellent as is the Thai-inspired spaghetti.

Above: bar area at the atmospheric Vine Wine Boutique Bar and Café

8. HANG GAI STREET SHOPPING *(see map, p26)*

Spend a morning shopping along Hang Gai, the capital's main tourist street. This itinerary highlights the best shops and art galleries along this street – renowned for its numerous silk and souvenir outlets – and includes forays into other streets leading off Hang Gai.

This route can be easily walked; when 'shopped-out', there is plenty of local transport on hand. Your starting point is at the beginning of Hang Gai Street, at the intersection with Hang Dao Street, just north of Hoan Kiem Lake; several refreshment stops are located nearby.

Hang Gai Street

The area directly north of Hoan Kiem Lake – to the east of Hang Dao Street – is known as **Tonkin Free Movement Square**, named after the short-lived patriotic group of 1907. This site was previously a 19th-century execution ground used by the French and a tramway station.

You now enter the retail republic of **Hang Gai Street**, the southern limit of the Old Quarter. Previously known as 'Hemp Street', ropes and jute were sold here in the old days, although later, wooden block printing became the main activity. During the 1946–47 Resistance War, the odd-numbered side of the street was under French control, while the even side came under the Vietnamese. Nowadays, so many silk tailor shops are concentrated on Hang Gai, it's become known as 'Silk Street'.

The first half of Hang Gai especially is unabashedly aimed at tourists and you'll find numerous silk shops selling modern and traditional silk clothes (such as the traditional female long dress called *ao dai*) – either tailor-made or off-the-rack – as well as silk bags, shoes, ties, scarves and sleeping bags. Most of the silk isn't 100 percent pure, but prices are generally low, tailoring services are good value and many products are simply gorgeous.

Countless souvenir shops in and around Hang Gai sell lacquerware, embroidery and other local craft products made from stone, wood and buffalo horn – as well as galleries selling Vietnamese contemporary and traditional art. This is the ideal place to buy a haul of souvenirs and gifts in one go, as well as getting something run up at the tailors (allow enough time for fittings and be very clear about your requirements).

If you are in need of caffeine before the onslaught, try a Vietnamese version of cappuccino at the hole-in-wall **Café Giang** (No 7) – it may lack ambience but locals swear by the coffee. One of Hanoi's best kept secrets is **Café Pho Co** (No 11), a café with a fourth-floor terrace that has great views over Hoan Kiem Lake. Or try **Little Hanoi** (Nos 21–23) – a delightful bar-café.

Right: entrance to Café Pho Co

At the intersection of Hang Gai and Luong Van Can, shops to your left sell cheap fake sunglasses; to your right, the stretch of **Luong Van Can Street** is known as 'Toy Street' for obvious reasons. Along Hang Gai at No 22, **Phuc Tin** is a family-run business selling hand-made, traditional silver jewellery. The craftsmanship and quality is some of the best in town; they can arrange tours to their workshop in the suburbs. At the top of **To Tich Alley**, a local street-side juice bar sells a refreshing concoction of fruit and vegetable juices, mixed with condensed or coconut milk.

Amongst numerous embroidery shops along Hang Gai, **Tan My** (No 66 and No 109) is one of the best. A family business established in 1968, Tan My has a good reputation for high quality, hand-made embroidered goods – including tablecloths, children's clothes and bedding – on top-notch cottons.

Established in the 1980s, upmarket **Khai Silk** (No 96) is Vietnam's most successful chain of silk boutiques, specialising in gorgeous silk clothes,

accessories and reliable tailoring services. Other good silk and tailor shops are **F Silk** (No 82) and **Kenly Silk** (No 108) – the latter's three-storey showcase store has a good range of hand-made silk garments and embroidered goods.

Its neighbour, **Green Palm Gallery**, is one of Hanoi's longer-established galleries for Vietnamese contemporary art. Just opposite, the innovative designer-owner of **Le Vent** (No 115) takes traditional Vietname designs and gives them a modern twist. Hand-made silk creations – sheer organza with detailed embroidery – including wall hangings, shawls and *ao dai* are good buys here.

Hang Bong Street

Hang Gai runs into **Hang Bong**, (formerly 'Cotton Street'), another good stretch for shopping. **Minh Tam** (No 2) sells traditional lacquerware as well as more contemporary black and white eggshell lacquerware. This family-run business will take customers to their lacquer workshop in a village outside Hanoi. Left is **Hang Trong Street**, which has more souvenir and craft shops, plus some interesting boutiques. On the corner, shops sell lacquered pictures of the fictional character Tin Tin – who the Vietnamese have taken a fancy to, for some reason – and water puppet figurines.

Continuing along Hang Bong, two small adjoining boutiques at No 16 – **Thang Long** and **Dzung** – are run by Vietnamese sisters who design and sell off-the-rack silk separates. **Salon Natasha** (No 30) was the first private art gallery in Hanoi, established in 1990 by Russian émigré Natasha and her Vietnamese artist husband. The gallery is actually the front room of the artist's home; the studio is a meeting place for artists and intellectuals and a venue for experimental and non-commercial art. Art works here are very different from mainstream Vietnamese contemporary art found elsewhere.

Above: interior of Kenly Silk Shop
Top right: wooden clogs at Pinocchio; **Right:** modern artwork at Salon Natasha

Tam Thuong Alley

At No 38, exit Hang Bong Street and enter a microcosm of Hanoi street life along **Tam Thuong Alley**. This quiet alley affords a quick breather from retail therapy, with numerous family guesthouses, miniscule food stalls and locals on their doorsteps washing dishes, gossiping and buying wares from street vendors.

The ancient **Yen Thai Communal House** (Dinh Yen Thai) – flanked by two gnarled banyan trees – is worth a look inside. Continue left into **Yen Thai Alley**. Previously specialising in embroidery, the founding patron of this area is worshipped at the nearby **Communal House** at No 2a. At the end of Yen Thai, exit onto Duong Thanh Street. On the opposite side of the road is **Hang Da Market** (Cho Hang Da), where piles of cheap, traditional ceramics are sold on the ground floor. Retrace your steps back to Hang Bong Street.

Apricot Gallery, at No 40b, is one of Hanoi's largest and most successful commercial art galleries, displaying works of leading contemporary Vietnamese artists and old masters. Even if you are not serious about buying, do go in and have a look around.

Also in this area, a concentration of shops sell Communist-style propaganda banners, flags, plaques and medals. **Pinocchio** (No 52 and No 122) sells hand-made, traditional Vietnamese wooden clogs adorned with silk straps and lacquered paint.

After all this, you may need some divine intervention: at No 120b, just inside an alley on your right, enter **Von Tien Temple** (Den Von Tien), an interesting little place of worship and hardly seen by tourists.

city itineraries

9. VIETNAMESE COOKERY CLASSES *(see map, p26)*

Learn the art of Vietnamese cuisine in a morning cookery class at the century-old Sofitel Metropole Hotel.

Classes are held daily at the Sofitel Metropole Hanoi Hotel, 15 Ngo Quyen Street, starting at 10am and lasting for about four hours. Bookings should be made at least one day in advance (04-826 6919, ext. 8110). The cost is about US$50, which includes lunch. A late afternoon cooking class with dinner is also available, and the morning class can be extended to include a trip to a noodle-making village or Bat Trang ceramics village (with an additional charge of US$30–40). Alternatively, there are several other cookery classes in Hanoi (see below).

Vietnamese food is fast becoming the hottest cuisine to emerge from Asia. Both the Chinese and French have heavily influenced Vietnamese cooking techniques, but the delicious dishes are as diverse as the country and rich in history – and unique in their own right. With an increasing interest and demand to learn about Vietnamese cuisine, the **Sofitel Metropole Hanoi Cookery School** opened in 1999 and has been a huge success ever since. Chefs from the hotel are especially assigned to the classes – overseen by its resident chef, Frenchman Didier Corlou.

To whet your appetite, the chef takes you first on an hour-long visit to one of Hanoi's oldest markets, **19–12 Market** (Cho 19–12). Top chefs in Hanoi – including those at the Metropole – swear by this open-air produce market. The two covered lanes of stalls are renowned for their quality fresh produce: fish, seafood, poultry, herbs and vegetables. The chef will buy some fresh produce at the market and introduce you to essential Vietnamese ingredients, explaining how to choose them carefully. The market itself has an interesting history *(see page 35 – Itinerary 3)*.

Above: a cookery class in progress at Sofitel Metropole Hotel

Back at the Sofitel Metropole, the chef performs an interactive cooking demonstration in the kitchen of the Spices Garden Restaurant. After watching the chef make it look oh-so-easy, it's now your turn, with a chance to create six different Vietnamese dishes – three traditional and three contemporary. These could include such dishes as marinated pork grilled in bamboo, banana flower salad or Hanoi deep-fried spring rolls. The best part is saved until last, with a chance to sample all the different dishes you prepared. After this, the heat is off and you can relax and enjoy a sit-down lunch with the other participants in the Spices Garden Restaurant – one of the finest Vietnamese restaurants in town.

Other Cookery Classes

Other cookery venues in town are also jumping on the increasingly popular Vietnamese culinary bandwagon. These offer tailor-made cookery classes, slightly more relaxed and informal than offered at the Metropole; prices depend on group size.

Moon River Retreat at Bac Cau 3, Ngoc Thuy Village, Long Bien District, is a charming riverside retreat, 5km (3 miles) from the centre of Hanoi (tel: 04-943 8896/090-450 9045). It offers tailor-made cookery classes for both guests and non-guests (minimum three people). A typical cookery class involves a trip to a local market, preparation and cooking from selected recipes with experienced Vietnamese chefs, then sitting down for lunch to sample the dishes.

Highway 4 at 54 Mai Hac De Street is a restaurant serving traditional North Vietnamese cuisine and liquor (contact Nuong, tel: 04-976 2589; e-mail: info@highway4.com). It offers a 'Be the Chef' class. Chefs from Highway 4 take you to a local market, then teach you how to prepare three traditional Vietnamese dishes in their kitchen – such as fish and coconut milk spring rolls – which you then sit down to taste. They also provide you with detailed recipes and cooking tips, so that you  can reproduce these dishes at home. Classes can be arranged daily from 9am–1pm (maximum six people).

Hidden Hanoi runs in-depth cultural tours in Hanoi (tel: 091 225 4045; e-mail: info@hiddenhanoi.com; www.hiddenhanoi.com). One of their tour options is a hands-on tailor-made Vietnamese cookery class in a local family home. Classes are flexible and last for four hours – maximum five people. After a visit to a market, you are given a menu sheet with instructions; under low-key supervision, you then prepare and cook traditional Hanoi family recipes, which you sit down and enjoy for lunch with your Vietnamese hosts. Geared to small groups wanting a more in-depth introduction to Vietnamese cuisine, a one-week course is offered also, which includes market visits and a recipe book.

Right: Highway 4 cookery class in progress

Excursions

The following excursions are either day trips or overnight excursions into the farther flung areas outside Hanoi city and its vicinity. The tours range from historic pagodas, fascinating craft villages and revered religious monuments on day tours from Hanoi to two- or three-day excursions to Halong Bay with its haunting scenery and Sapa, an atmospheric hill station dating back to French rule.

1. TAY PHUONG, THAY AND TRAM GIAN PAGODAS, AND VAN PHUC *(see map, p58)*

Tay Phuong, Thay and Tram Gian pagodas offer rich history and old architecture amidst tranquil, rural scenery; a visit to Van Phuc silk village rounds the day off.

Set off early at around 7.30am. The two main attractions – Thay and Tay Phuong pagodas – can be a morning tour by themselves. Some Hanoi tour operators run the pagodas as a day tour, with other attractions en route. You'll get the most from this tour with a knowledgeable guide and in a small group. Exotissimo and Buffalo Tours can arrange a private tour (US$45–50 per person for two), inclusive of driver, car, picnic lunch, guide and entrance fees. The trip can also be done by motorbike. The first stop is Tay Phuong Pagoda, about 25km (15½ miles) west of Hanoi in Thac Xa village, Ha Tay Province. Some climbing is involved, and bring a torch.

Tay Phuong Pagoda

Tay Phuong Pagoda (Chua Tay Phuong, or 'Pagoda of the West') is found 50m (160ft) atop a limestone hill. You need to climb some 239 worn steps to get to it, but your efforts will be rewarded with the sight of a beautifully constructed low-rise pagoda. One of the oldest pagodas in Vietnam – the site allegedly dating back to the 3rd century – Tay Phuong was renovated in the 17th and 18th centuries.

Built of ironwood with bare brick walls and round windows, Tay Phuong has three connected sections – the Three Gems (Tam Bao). Its exquisite double and curved roofs – typical of the north – are richly decorated with engraved wood edges and terracotta dragons and phoenixes. The pagoda is famed for over 70 wonderfully preserved wooden statues, including eight *dharma* guardians, but most notably for its 18 *arhats* (monks who have reached nirvana), grouped at the rear. An outstanding example of 18th-century sculpture, they portray in great detail various forms of human expression.

Left: steps leading up to Tay Phuong Pagoda
Right: an *arhat* statue at Tay Phuong Pagoda

Thay Pagoda

Return to the highway, turn left and continue for 2km (1¼ miles). Just before the tollbooth, at a large sign for 'Chua Thay' on your right, turn left, continuing for 3km (1¾ miles). **Thay Pagoda** (Chua Thay or 'Master's Pagoda') is actually a complex founded in 1132 (renovated in the 17th century), set amid a picturesque lake, village and limestone hills. Also known as 'Heavenly Blessing Pagoda', it is dedicated to the cult of 'Master' Tu Dao Hanh, a revered Buddhist monk who lived here. Tu was a skilled herbalist who cured many locals and kept them entertained with water puppet shows performed on the lake pavilion. Some believe he was the founder of this art form. From the fifth to the seventh day of the third lunar month, traditional water puppetry is performed for the thousands of pilgrims who gather here.

The **main pagoda** has three low-rise sections. The highest represents Tu Dao Hanh's three reincarnations, with three altars. To your left is a statue of his time as King Ly Than Tong and in the centre, a 13th-century statue of his *bodhisattva* form. The right-hand altar represents Tu the monk, with a photograph of his puppet-like wooden statue. The actual statue is brought out, washed and displayed for only three days a year, at a spe-

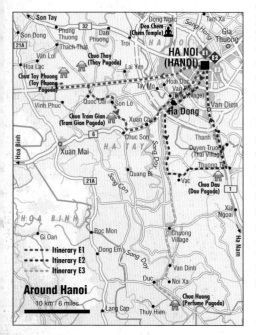

Above: Moon Bridge, Thay Pagoda

cial festival. The **middle section**, dedicated to Buddha, has some striking statues, notably two enormous guardians – one benevolent and one fierce, reflecting Yin and Yang elements – and eight smaller guardians, flanking a central altar crowded with wooden statues. Eighteen *arhats* are displayed outside, along the sides of the pagoda, although they aren't as impressive as those at Tay Phuong.

Two arched, covered bridges spanning the lake were built in 1602. **Sun Bridge** leads to a small islet temple; the other, **Moon Bridge**, leads to steep stone steps ascending to **Mountain Pagoda**, where Tu Dao Hanh led his monk's life. This peaceful spot offers good views and is ideal for picnics. Amid the shrines, a small grotto –**Thanh Hoa** – is where Tu meditated and died. To the rear of the pagoda, a precarious trail over rocks leads to several grottoes, including **Cac Co**; unless you have a fascination with grottoes, they aren't worth the effort.

Tram Gian Pagoda

Turning back onto the highway, take the narrow road immediately opposite, which leads to **Tram Gian Pagoda**. En route, you'll pass picturesque rural scenery and **Quoc Oai village** – the pagoda is roughly 8km (5 miles) south of here. As well as its interesting architectural style, Tram Gian Pagoda is worth visiting for its idyllic rural setting – perched on top of a hill, surrounded by trees and with lovely views.

Tram Gian – dating from the 12th century– is known as the '100 Compartment Pagoda' (Chua Tram Gian). If each group of ironwood columns is considered a compartment, the low-rise pagoda has 104, divided into three sections. The **main pagoda** houses 153 statues, including that of a 14th-century resident monk – later called St Boi. He is credited with several miracles, including blood-like rains that drowned invading Chinese troops. Legend has it that this statue is his actual body, embalmed and covered with lacquer. The pagoda is flanked by stupas containing the ashes of former 'Master' monks and in front, a bell tower, which can be climbed.

Van Phuc Silk Village

Drive towards Highway 6, roughly 3km (1¾ miles) from here. Turn left in the direction of Hanoi; at the Ha Dong intersection, around 11km (6¾ miles) from Hanoi, turn left for **Van Phuc** just after the post office (*buu dien*). You'll soon encounter two entrances for Van Phuc on your right. Families in Van Phuc have been producing silk for centuries, but it is only within the last decade that the glut of retail shops lining the main street have sprung up. Many proprietors own silk shops along Hanoi's Hang Gai Street, or sell their silks there; naturally prices are generally lower in Van Phuc. As well as ordering and buying silk, you can wander into the workshops to watch silk being woven. Old-fashioned electric silk looms introduced by the French in the early 20th century are still used.

Right: silk weavers at Van Phuc

2. TRADITIONAL CRAFT VILLAGES *(see map, p58)*

A day visiting traditional villages that produce conical hats, birdcages, fans and lacquerware, plus an ancient pagoda with mummified statues. The route passes typical Red River Delta countryside, affording glimpses of timeless village life.

Dozens of craft villages surround Hanoi. Many tour operators run day tours to a selection, but this excursion visits less touristed villages. Hire a car (or motorbike) and guide through a reputable tour company (see page 100). Take a picnic lunch – although there's a decent local soup kitchen en route. Set off early; the first stop is Chuong Village (Thanh Oai District, Ha Tay Province). Chuong Village (also known as Phuong Trung) is roughly 13km (8 miles) along Highway 21b/60; a large sign on the left and right ('Lang Chuong, Xa Phuong Truong') indicates the village entrance.

Chuong Village

The conical hat (*non la*) is the typical headgear used by Vietnamese women, especially in the countryside, protecting them from rain and sun. There are many types of conical hats – solid and thick for farm work and everyday use, or thinner and more elegant for decorative purposes – **Chuong Village** specialises mostly in the former. Another variety, with a stencilled poem inserted between the hat's layers, is produced mainly in Hue, Central Vietnam.

Although a simple concept, making a conical hat is a skilled process, consisting of a framework of thin bamboo hoops, covered with palm (*non*) leaves. A conical frame is used to create the main base of the hat, with the leaves meticulously sewn into place over this. This is a home-based industry, with the whole village involved in one way or another. Everywhere you wander, you'll see women at various stages of hat production – usually in their front yards. You'll also see palm leaves drying out in the sun: these

Above: Vietnamese conical hats being created at Chuong Village

are then separated, whitened with sulphur and flattened with an iron, before stitched into the hats.

Locals are friendly and – like all the villages on this excursion – will not mind you watching them at work. A hat here costs roughly 20,000d, usually taking one day to produce. Many are for export, although some are for sale locally. The joy of this village is simply to wander down lanes and glimpse traditional work and village life. Also worth visiting is the **Catholic church** (if locked, ask one of the locals to let you in for a small 'donation') and amidst the village market, an old **communal house** (*dinh*). Part of the *dinh* was destroyed by French bombs, but it is now undergoing restoration – note the intricate word carvings and festival palanquins. Nearby is a well-preserved '**Women's Pagoda**', with several resident nuns. A village festival falls on the 10th day of the first lunar month.

Vac Village

Vac Village – known as birdcage village – is 3km (1¾ miles) away. Return to the main road and turn right. After roughly 2km (1¼ miles), turn left at the sign 'Di Uoc Le'; Vac is a short distance to the right. Bamboo birdcages of all shapes and sizes are hand-produced here; some ornate with carved bases and intricate designs. Wander through narrow lanes to see the villagers working at their front yards. Some families also make bamboo slats, used for traditional shoulder pole baskets.

Hand-made paper fans are also produced at Vac Village. You can see the entire fan production process; pots of indigo ink for dyeing the paper, and the basic bamboo frames which form the base of the fans – sometimes decorated with buffalo horn. A simple, hand-held needle creates fine hole patterns on the fan. Fans generally cost 1,000–5,000d; many are produced for export.

Back on the main road, turn right (in the direction you were heading before) for **Thuong Tin** town. If you want to go native for lunch, make a stop at **Thuong Tin**. Numerous street kitchens on the right, including Minh Phuong's Pho Bo at No 326, serve tasty beef noodle soup.

Dau Pagoda's Mummified Monks

Alternatively, **Dau Pagoda** (Chua Dau) is a lovely picnic spot. To get there, before you reach Thuong Tin, turn right at the sign for Chua Dau. Continue along for a while; at a blue sign just before a bridge – and at Nha Tiep Linh prayer building – turn left and the road brings you to Dau Pagoda.

This delightful pagoda – framed by a lake and river – dates back to the 12th century. Its three-entrance gate also serves as a bell tower – climb up to view the bronze bell. The square complex consists of a front ceremonial hall complete with intricate woodcarvings; two parallel corridors, passing a central altar, lead to a rear building. Inside, glass cases display the 'statues' of 17th-century monks, Vu Khac Minh and Vu Khac Truong. These are in fact

Right: Vac Village specialises in the making of bamboo bird cages

the lacquered mummified skeletal remains of two brothers who died meditating – scientists have verified their authenticity. Dau Pagoda is also a regional Buddhism school; a small sanctuary includes a library, where x-ray photographs of the statues support their authenticity.

Duyen Truong Village

Head back into Thuong Tin; at the T-junction and railway tracks turn left into Highway 1, heading for Hanoi. Drive past a 'Hanoi 17km' marker; just past the Coca-Cola factory, turn right at the next main street and keep driving until the end of road (and the new elevated highway in front). You are now in **Duyen Truong Village**, which specialises in lacquerware products. Stroll around the village and wander into family workshops to see the whole lacquer process (*see pages 77–8*). Unfinished lacquerware pieces are strewn around front yards in various stages of production. Decorated votive paper boxes used for ceremonial burning are also made here. A lacquer factory (on the other side of the new highway) churns out high-quality lacquer products for big export orders.

3. PERFUME PAGODA *(see map, p58)*

A full day, taking a boat ride through riverine karst scenery and a climb to the top of a mountain to experience one of Vietnam's largest and most important religious sites.

Make an early start as you will be travelling 60km (37¼ miles) southwest of Hanoi, the journey comprising three parts: by road, by boat and a 4km (2½ miles) 'mountain' hike. Most Hanoi tour operators (see page 100) run this tour with lunch, entrance fees, transport and guide included in the price; other attractions are sometimes visited en route. During the first two months after Tet (Feb/Mar or Mar/Apr depending on the lunar calendar), the site

can get very crowded with pilgrims, making for a frustrating (or alternatively, highly interesting) experience. The walk up the mountain is steep and can be quite tough going; wear sensible shoes and bring lots of water. In the summer, it can get very hot. Boats have no cover, so bring sun protection. And bring a torch for the poorly lit caves.

The **Perfume Pagoda** (Chua Huong) is one of the largest and most important religious sites in

Above: lacquerware at Duyen Truong
Left: paddling up Yen River

Vietnam (daily 7.30am–6pm). It's just one of dozens of pagodas and Buddhist shrines – the earliest dating from the 15th century – covering an area of 30sq km (11½sq miles) and built into the limestone cliffs of **Huong Tich Mountain** (Mountain of the Fragrant Traces). This area was the site of some bitter uprisings against the French colonialists, and as a result, several of the pagodas and shrines were destroyed during the late 1940s.

This sacred site is extremely important to Vietnamese pilgrims who converge here from the start of the first lunar month (just after Tet) to the middle of the third lunar month – the annual spring festival period. Many devout Buddhists will attempt to visit this shrine at least once in their lifetime.

Boat Trip and a Hike

The journey by road brings you to riverside **Duc Village**: from the boat station, low-level, metal-bottomed boats transport you to the Perfume Pagoda complex (there are no roads into the area). To some, the one and a half-hour boat trip along the wide, swiftly flowing **Yen River** is almost as worthwhile as visiting the pagoda itself. The boats – deftly rowed by local oarswomen – glide past verdant rice paddy landscape studded with jagged limestone karst hills, reminiscent of the scenery in China's Guilin area. The peace and serenity of the journey is only interrupted when you disembark at the base of Huong Tich Mountain for the start of the one- to two-hour climb.

You first pass an unholy glut of souvenir and food stalls before reaching your first stop, the 17th-century **Pagoda Leading to Heaven** (Chua Thien Tru) – or the 'Outer Pagoda'. In front stands a stunning triple-roofed bell tower; to the side, the start of well-defined stone steps worn smooth with the passage of time – these ascend to the heavens and the 'Inner Pagoda''.

As well as passing various shrines and pagodas en route, punctuated by bonus views of forests and mountains, the stepped route is littered with an assortment of vendors selling snacks and Buddhist trinkets. Development plans for the future include cable cars to ferry pilgrims to the top, so in the

Above: Perfume Pagoda area

future it may not be necessary to walk. This slightly defeats the purpose, however, as the whole point of the pilgrimage is overcoming challenges to get there! The hassle from over-enthusiastic child vendors on the way up may well be enough to drive you prayers.

The **Pagoda of the Perfumed Vestige** (Huong Tich Chua), or the 'Inner Pagoda', is located inside the **Huong Tich Grotto**, which lies just below the summit of the mountain. Some 120 stone steps bedecked with Buddhist flags lead down to the 'dragon's mouth' entrance. Chinese characters etched on the outside of the cave declare that you are entering 'the most beautiful grotto under the southern sky'. In the darkness of the 50-m (160-ft) high cave, surrounded by stalactites and stalagmites, are numerous gilded Buddhist statues with altar offerings of fruit and incense. Numerous flickering candles and a haze of incense smoke lend added atmosphere to the place. Found centrestage is an image of **Quan Am** – Goddess of Mercy and the female personification of Buddha. Legend has it that *bodhisatttva* Avalokiteshvara transformed himself here into the female deity Quan Am. The shrine is now dedicated to her (or him).

Some visitors find the pagoda a bit of an anti-climax after all the effort it takes to get here (especially after battling the crowds at festival time). Although the Perfume Pagoda is pretty low-key, it is an important and sacred Buddhist pilgrimage site and the cave – gloriously cool from the outside heat – emanates a sense of serenity and holiness.

The return boat trip not only affords a second opportunity to drink in the mesmerising scenery that so inspired Vietnamese poets, but also the chance to rest weary limbs after the descent.

Above: interior of Huong Tich Grotto
Left: Pagoda of the Perfumed Vestige

excursions

4. TAM COC, BICH DONG AND PHAT DIEM CATHEDRAL *(see map, p66)*

A full day, with a sampan ride through Tam Coc's waterlogged karst landscape, a visit to a cave-pagoda, then on to the 19th-century architectural wonder, Phat Diem Cathedral.

A long day, departing Hanoi at 6am and returning around 7pm. Most tour companies combine Tam Coc and Bich Dong with Hoa Lu – site of an ancient citadel and former capital – this excursion features Phat Diem Cathedral instead. Arrange a car and guide with Buffalo Tours or Exotissimo (see page 100) – around US$60–65 per person for two, with picnic lunch and entrance fees. The first stop is Tam Coc, 99km (61½ miles) from Hanoi: which entails a drive and a boat trip. There's no shade on the boats, so bring sun protection. Phat Diem is a further 39km (24¼ miles) southeast. Free tours of the cathedral by seminarians are recommended, but limited – book in advance from the office outside the cathedral gates (daily 7.30–11.30am, 2.30–5pm; tel: 030-862 058), or secure on arrival. A donation is appreciated.

Tam Coc

Prepare for a few hours of idyllic scenery and tranquillity at **Tam Coc**, as you set off in your small sampan – complete with local oarswoman. The boat meanders past jagged limestone rocks jutting out of a landscape of flooded rice paddies merging with Ngo Dong River – a mystical scene forever immortalised in the film *Indochine*. With the same geological formations rising from the water, Tam Coc is invariably declared 'a land-locked Halong Bay' and can get just as busy – sometimes with a long posse of boats full of tourists snaking their way along the river.

Tam Coc means '**Three Caves**' and you actually pass under three, long, low-hanging tunnel caves – the largest complete with stalactites and stalagmites – that have bored through the limestone hills over the centuries. Clear lagoons, darting kingfishers and locals scouring for shellfish complete the rural scenario: the only slap of reality is the hassling by boat crews to purchase local merchandise. The best tack is simply to ignore them (some tour guides pay the touts not to bother them); allegedly, the government is trying to crack down on this tourism scourge.

On the return, stop at the 13th-century **Thai Vi Temple** – a short stroll from the banks – where King Tran Nhan Tong retired after his abdication.

Bich Dong Cave-Pagoda

Jade Grotto, better known as **Bich Dong Cave-Pagoda**, is 2km (1¼ miles) southwest of the boat wharf. At the pagoda entrance, stone steps hewn into a limestone rock dotted with shrines lead up to a cave entrance where three Buddhas sit atop lotus thrones. Walk through here and climb further up the cliff face steps, where there are more Buddhist shrines and a terrace with stunning valley views.

Right: Tam Coc oarswoman in the rain

Phat Diem Cathedral

Phat Diem Cathedral is one of Vietnam's architectural masterpieces, yet is surprisingly little frequented by tourists (daily 7–11am, 2–5pm; mass daily 5am and 5pm; Sun, 5am, 9.30am, 4pm; if buildings are locked, find someone with a key to open up). Constructed from ironwood, marble and granite, it is the only Catholic cathedral in Vietnam officially certified by the government. Vietnamese Catholics constitute the largest Catholic group in Southeast Asia, apart from the Philippines.

Travelling south from Ninh Binh for 30km (18¾ miles), you pass through

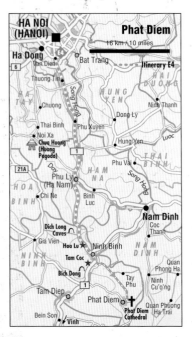

'Catholic country' – with numerous churches and distant spires scattered across rice fields. Catholic graveyards line the road, their white, coffin-shaped tombs sinking into the marshy ground. Sixty-five parishes belong to Phat Diem, with nearly a church in every village. Pre-1954, 90 percent of the parish congregation was Catholic. From 1954 to 1980, however, Catholicism was forbidden in the region and 60,000 locals – including more than 100 priests – fled to the Ho Chi Minh City region. Today, only 33 per cent of the area's population are Catholic.

Covering over 2 hectares (5 acres), the Phat Diem complex consists of a main cathedral, five separate chapels, three grottoes and a bell tower, set before a small lake. Phat Diem is particularly noteworthy for its unique style of architecture, stunning

Above: Phat Diem Cathedral

the onlooker on arrival – a combination of Oriental Buddhist pagoda and European Gothic. The main architectural characteristics are boxy cupolas with overhanging curved roofs, but with telltale crosses adorning the top. This may have something to do with its Vietnamese architect, Catholic priest and visionary Father Tran Luc – known as Father Six – who blended his Christian beliefs with European and traditional Vietnamese cultures. His tomb lies in the church courtyard.

The **Bell Tower** (Phuong Dinh) is an imposing stone square structure, reflected in the water. The last monument of the complex to be built, it resembles a Vietnamese communal house and has no doors. Climb to the top for views of churches dotted across the region, as well as the coastline and mountains. When resounded, the tower's 2-ton (2032-kg) bronze bell can be heard for over 10km (6¼ miles).

The even more stunning **Phat Diem Cathedral** lies behind. Within its tranquil, dim interior, the nave extends for 74m (240ft) and is supported by 52 iron wood pillars, 16 of which are 11-m (36-ft) high. The front sanctuary area above the single slab altar is decorated with Orthodox-style lacquered and gilded carved woodwork. Note the angels with Vietnamese faces near the vaulted ceiling. Surrounding the cathedral are the **Bishop's House**, three grottoes and five chapels – **Stone Chapel** (also known as the Immaculate Heart) is, as the name suggests, made entirely of stone.

Phat Diem Cathedral is all the more remarkable for the way it was built. It took 14 years and was completed in 1899 – ironically the year of Father Six's death. This area previously comprised reed swamps, not populated until 1829 – although European Catholic missionaries had been arriving here by sea since the 16th century. To secure the foundations, bamboo stakes were driven 30m (98ft) into the ground, topped by earth, rock and bamboo mats.

The materials used – stone, timber and marble – all came from afar by waterway as none were available locally. Sand and lime were used as mortar and ramps of earth were used as leverage, then spread over the site – explaining why the ground level is higher than the surrounding land. The builders obviously did a good job: along with the ravages of time, unsuitable building location and war damage during the French and American wars (1953 and 1972 respectively), the cathedral has held up remarkably well, although the complex has undergone extensive restorations.

The surrounding villages are renowned for sedge mat production – mats are laid out to dry by the side of the road. You'll have plenty of opportunity to purchase sedge products, as well as see the whole weaving process.

Right: Catholic worshippers at Phat Diem Cathedral

5. HALONG BAY *(see map, p70)*

A few days cruising around Halong Bay – one of the most magnificent natural splendours of Asia. Swathed in legends and beauty and only three hours from Hanoi, this World Heritage Site should not be missed.

The best way to appreciate Halong Bay is by boat. This is one destination where it pays to go on an organised tour (see details below). Almost every Hanoi tour operator arranges one- to four-day boat tours of the bay, in vessels ranging from Chinese junk-style boats to a luxury replica French paddle steamer. Generally, the tours offer a package of meals, guide, boat (with accommodation on board) and transfers. Unscrupulous boat owners in Halong City are notorious for ripping off tourists so forget about doing this trip on your own. Boats depart daily from Bai Chay Tourist Wharf in Halong City, 165km (102 miles) east of Hanoi by road. For those with limited time, there are one-day tours with roughly four hours cruising, but this is not a feasible option given the three-hour road journey to Halong City.

The best time to visit Halong is in warmer weather from April to October as you can swim off the boat and relax on sundecks. However, during the typhoon season which peaks in August *(see page 89)* boats may cancel due to bad weather. Between January and March, the weather can be cool and drizzly but even then

Above and left: the *Huong Hai* Chinese-style junk at Halong Bay

Halong Bay can be a pleasurable experience – the swirling mists that swaddle the magnificent limestone outcrops lend an ethereal beauty to it.

There may be karst formations elsewhere (Thailand's Phang Nga Bay for instance), but few could fail to be impressed with Halong Bay (Vinh Ha Long); over 3,000 limestone islands jutting out of emerald green waters in the Gulf of Tonkin. In an area covering 1,500sq km (579sq miles), sampans, junks, fishing boats – and numerous tourist boats – sail past a fairy-tale backdrop of mostly uninhabited limestone karsts – which yield grottoes, secluded coves, coral beaches and hidden lagoons. No wonder UNESCO designated this area a World Heritage Site in 1994. Even in poor weather the mist-shrouded limestone outcrops seem to accentuate the bay's mythical beauty.

A Load of New Junk

All tour operators use engine-powered wooden boats, some with private cabins – although you can sleep on deck (highly recommended). Many are built to resemble Chinese junks complete with red sails. Although tours are generally cheap, boats can get crowded. A new breed of upmarket luxury junk boats has recently emerged, with top-notch dining, large sundecks, elegant en-suite cabins and international-style service.

Buffalo Tours (tel: 04-828 0702; www.buffalotours.com) have their own *Jewel of the Bay* luxury junk with five en-suite cabins for two- to three-day tours (from US$120). **Handspan** (tel: 04-933 2377, www.handspan.com) use the *Dragon's Pearl* junk with 18 en-suite cabins on two- or three-day options (from US$70); kayaks are available on both boats. **Exotissimo** (tel: 04-828 2150; www.exotissimo.com) run cruises on board the *Huong Hai* Chinese junk with kayaking and beach camping options. **Emeraude Classic Cruises** (tel: 04-934 0888; www.emeraude-cruises.com) operate a luxury replica of the single-wheeled paddle steamers used by the French a century ago: two-day cruises cost US$290 per cabin.

The Stuff of Legends

Halong Bay's awesome scenery looks the stuff of legends – which it is. Ha Long means 'Descending Dragon', originating from the myth that a celestial dragon once flung herself headlong into the sea, her swishing tail digging deep valleys and crevices in the mainland. As she descended into the sea, these filled with water, creating the bay.

According to another legend, the Jade Emperor ordered a dragon to halt an invasion by sea from the north. The dragon spewed out jade and jewels which upon hitting the sea turned into wondrous islands and karst formations, creating a natural fortress against enemy ships. The dragon was so enchanted by her creations that she decided to stay in the bay. To this day, local fishermen swear that they have spotted the shape of a dragon-like creature in the waters.

Right: replica old-world paddle steamer operated by Emeraude Classic Cruises

Throughout history, Halong Bay was the downfall of many marauding invaders. General Ngo Quyen defeated Chinese forces in 938 by embedding hundreds of iron tipped stakes in the Bach Dang River, then luring the fleet upstream in high tide. He then attacked as the tide turned, driving the Chinese downstream and onto the exposed stakes. Incredibly, four centuries later, in 1288, Kublai Khan fell for the same ruse, this time masterminded by General Tran Hung Dao.

Islands and Grottoes

Legends aside, geologists believe that the karst outcrops were formed by a giant limestone sea bed, eroding until only pinnacles remained behind. Locals named them after the shapes they resemble: teapot, toad, elephant's foot, etc. Over the centuries, elements within the rock slowly dissolved by rain formed hundreds of bizarre-shaped grottoes; around 15 now open to the public.

Boats usually visit a couple of caves en route; tickets are purchased at the Tourist Wharf. The most well-known is found on the island nearest to Halong City – **Grotto of Wooden Stakes** (Hang Dau Go) – where General Tran Hung Dao amassed hundreds of stakes prior to his 1288 victory. On the same island, the **Grotto of the Heavenly Palace** (Hang Thien Cung) has some impressive stalactites and stalagmites, as does **Surprise Grotto**

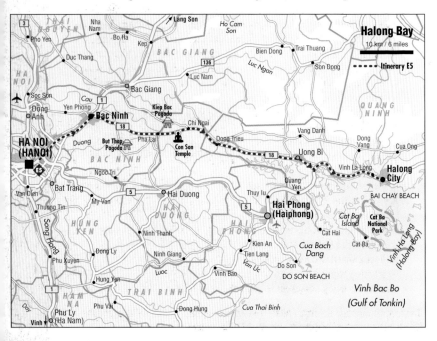

(Hang Sung Sot) on an island further south. **Hang Hanh** is a tunnel cave that extends for 2km (1¼ miles); access by sampan is strictly regulated by tides. **Three Tunnel Lake** (Ho Ba Ham), a shallow lagoon surrounded by limestone walls on Dau Bo Island, can only be reached by navigating three low tunnels at low tide.

Cat Ba Island

Cat Ba Island, the largest in Halong Bay at 354 sq km (136 sq miles), offers spectacular, rugged landscape – forested limestone peaks, offshore coral reefs, coastal mangrove and freshwater swamps, lakes and waterfalls. Almost half the island and adjacent waters are a national park, with diverse flora and fauna. You can trek through here, cruise through **Lan Ha Bay** or Halong Bay itself. Although the island is dotted with a few villages, **Cat Ba town** is the main settlement – some boats dock in the fishing harbour, where mini-hotels and basic tourist services are located. Although tourism plays an increasingly dominant role, Cat Ba is still a fishing community.

Many tourist boats spend one or two nights here, or visit the national park. Despite Cat Ba Island being overrun in the summer with numerous tourist boats in the vicinity, Halong Bay is still a peaceful spot. However, several tour companies now sail further east into **Bai Tu Long Bay** in search of more solitude. Bai Tu Long's little-frequented islands such as **Quan Lan Island** – with sweeping deserted beaches and welcoming fishing communities – are now the area's worst kept secret.

Top left: fisherman at a grotto altar; **Above:** Halong Bay can be idyllic even when it's enveloped in mist; **Right:** kayaking at Cat Ba Island

6. SAPA *(see map, p74)*

A former French hill station near the Chinese border, Sapa offers breath-taking mountain scenery, trekking and close encounters with ethnic minorities. Aim for at least two full days here.

Every Hanoi tour operator (see page 100) organises tours to Sapa – from one to several nights – with guide, transport and accommodation, and a choice of tours included. Sapa, 360km (223 miles) northwest of Hanoi, is one of the relatively few easy destinations for independent travellers, but make sure you book your return train ticket (and hotel) in advance. Trains can get very full, especially at weekends. Night trains (soft-sleeper four-berths with fan or air-conditioning cost US$12–16 one way; for more comfort, book the Tulico berths, tel: 04-828 7806; www.tulico-sapa.com) depart daily from Tran Quy Cap station (behind the main station on Le Duan Street) at 10pm, arriving at Lao Cai station the following morning at 6–7am. Sapa hotels can organise transfers from Lao Cai but there also tourist minibuses (tickets cost 25,000d) which await incoming trains for the 39-km (24¼-mile) drive to Sapa. If money is no object, book a package with the Victoria Sapa Hotel, which also transfers guests on board its luxurious Victoria Express Train (see details below).

The best time to visit is September to November and March to May. The rainy summer months, particularly July and August, are Sapa's busiest months (with the most expensive hotel rates), when Hanoians flock here to escape the heat. Temperatures can plummet in winter, with frost and occasional snow, so be sure to book a room with adequate heating. Nighttime temperatures are low throughout the year, so bring warm clothing. The weather, however, can be variable all year: blazing hot, then low cloud, then rain and fog suddenly rolling in. Weekends – especially peak summer months – can get very crowded; weekdays are more relaxed, and room rates are lower.

Above: rice terraces surrounding Sapa

Hill Station History

The French had the right idea when they made Sapa their hill station in the first half of the 20th century. With its similarity to the Alps, its cool climate – at 1,600m (5,249 ft) – was a welcome refuge from the stifling humidity and reminded them of home. As you zig-zag your way uphill from Lao Cai – with spectacular views of terraced rice fields and the breathtaking Hoang Lien Son mountain range – bear in mind that the French colonialists were carried up here by sedan chair. Dramatically perched on the edge of a high plateau (along with most of the hotels), Sapa has a stunning location, framed by soaring blue peaks and sweeping valleys dotted with paddy fields and ethnic minority villages. Relaxing on your balcony – with Mount Fansipan almost within touching distance – it doesn't get much better than this.

Lying forgotten for approximately half a century– until another invasion of foreigners rediscovered it in the 1990s – Sapa is currently undergoing major tourism development, with a number of new hotels under construction. It may have lost a little of its soul, yet Sapa is still charming and the perfect base to explore stupendous outlying scenery and ethnic minority villages, where traditional daily life carries on as it has done for centuries.

Sapa's Hotels

Tourist buses from Lao Cai terminate in Sapa's town centre. Recommended hotels in Sapa are the luxury four-star **Victoria Sapa Hotel** (tel: 020-871 522; www.victoriahotels-asia.com), Sapa's first international standard hotel, which has a good restaurant called Ta Van and a huge, open lobby fireplace. Guests can book the exclusive Victoria Express overnight train, a romantic and classic way to travel, departing four times a week. Package deals from US$217 include train, hotel, tours, meals and transfers.

Other hotels include the long-established, rustic **Auberge Dang Trung** (Cau May Street, tel: 020-871 243; www.sapadiscovery.com); which has a decent restaurant and an owner with sound local knowledge of the area, and **Sapa Goldsea** (58 Fansipan Road, tel: 020-872180; e-mail: sapagoldsea@ hn.vnn.vn), a new medium-range hotel. **Baguette & Chocolat Sapa** (Thac Bac Street, tel: 020-871 766; e-mail: hoasuaschoolsp@hn.vnn.vn) has four delightful rooms above their restaurant-café-bakery, serving delicious goodies and picnic baskets for your highland treks.

Ethnic Minorities

Nearly two-thirds of Vietnam's ethnic minority groups live in the northern mountainous regions – hence the name 'Le Montagnards'. Each with their own distinctive dress, customs and dialects, they subsist mostly through farming – rice and maize – cultivated on terraced fields. Sapa's main groups are the Giay, Tay, Xa Pho, but predominantly the Black Hmong and Red Dao. The Black Hmong are totally at ease with foreigners, and are recognisable

Right: a Flower Hmong trader at Bac Ha market, near Sapa.

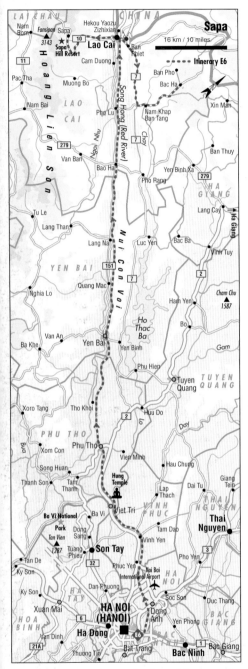

by their indigo-blue hemp attire. Many Hmong females are excellent local guides, speak good English and have savvy sales techniques. On the streets of Sapa, they literally mob tourists with their handicraft wares. The Red Dao (pronounced 'Zao'), are generally much shyer but more striking with their scarlet turban-style headdress, embroidered clothes and often, shaved head and eyebrows.

Trekking

The main reason to come to Sapa is the opportunity to trek through ethnic minority villages, staying overnight in local stilt houses – especially since government restrictions have been lifted. Several outlying villages – **Cat Cat**, **Ta Van**, **Sin Chai**, **Lao Chai** and **Ta Phin** – make pleasant and relatively easy treks. However, as these villages are becoming increasingly commercialised, many operators are now venturing further afield, hiking to more remote mountain villages and scenery.

Try and trek with a local guide, as they understand the local dialects, etiquette and customs better and are able to explain a good deal more. Bring good walking boots, repellant, water and medical kit and as the weather is variable – sunscreen, hat, waterproofs and warm clothing. In settlements, always ask first before taking photographs; dress modestly and respect local customs.

Recommended local tour operators include **Topas Adventure Vietnam** (11 Cau May Street, tel: 020-871331; Hanoi branch at 29 Hang Giay, tel: 04-928 3637; www.topas-adventure-vietnam.com) and the aforementioned **Auberge Dang Trung**. Both offer trekking, horse riding, mountain biking and other options; which some Hanoi-based operators also offer (*see page 100*).

Right: the Sapa Market becomes especially lively on weekends

Ethnic Markets

In the recent past, Sapa used to be sold on the pretext of a Saturday night '**Love Market**', where young minorities coyly met potential suitors in the town centre. This form of voyeuristic tourism, however, has been stopped by the authorities and the tradition has moved to a more secluded area.

However, the **Sapa Market** in central Sapa is worth investigating (weekends are especially lively) as are a number of fascinating but remote weekly ethnic minority markets – located several hours from Sapa – which offer more traditional market life. **Can Cau** (Saturday), **Coc Ly** (Tuesday) and **Muong Hom** (Sunday), all found near the Chinese border, are highly recommended; arrange a tour or hire a jeep (roughly US$50–60) through local operators. Colourful, vibrant **Bac Ha Market** starts early Sunday morning in Bac Ha – roughly 80km (50 miles) east of Sapa. Operators run this as a day trip and can drop you at Lao Cai train station on the return trip to Sapa.

Mount Fansipan

Looming ominously over Sapa, **Mount Fansipan** entices the more adventurous – and fit – to conquer its summit, which, with the right conditions, is possible. Standing at 3,143m (10,311ft) in the middle of **Hoang Lien Son Nature Reserve**, Vietnam's (and Indochina's) highest mountain offers stunning panoramic views. Not so much technically demanding, Fansipan is still a challenging experience. Located 5km (3 miles) as the crow flies, the climb can take several days up steep, overgrown trails – very much dependant on variable weather conditions. This is not recommended in rainy weather, when conditions are not only difficult, but also extremely treacherous.

If you decide to make the ascent to Mount Fansipan, make sure that you arrange the trip with experienced operators *(see pages 74 and 100)*, who offer two- to four-day packages with all the necessary equipment (porters, guides, tents and cooking facilities). If weather conditions look bad – and the weather here can be very erratic – they will cancel the trip.

Leisure Activities

SHOPPING

Hanoi is a shopper's paradise, but in some respects it is woefully underdeveloped compared with other Asian capitals. Although making great strides since the 1990s, Hanoi has only a few small shopping arcades, no large department stores, few designer boutiques and a limited range of consumer goods. But perhaps that's its beauty, especially if sanitised and glitzy shopping malls are anathema to you.

Vietnam has its own distinctive, unique range of traditional handicrafts and goods, especially silks, lacquerware and embroidery. Old 'tube houses' and colonial villas are the perfect setting for Hanoi's traditional artistic heritage – many shops are as beautiful as the products sold. The main tourist shopping areas are in the **Old Quarter**: around St Joseph's Cathedral; Hang Gai Street and the backpacker-orientated Dinh Liet, Hang Bac, Ma May and Hang Be streets.

It's also worth browsing in local markets such as **Cho Dong Xuan** and traditional craft villages outside Hanoi. Shopping is ridiculously cheap: smarter establishments have fixed prices, but many places sell goods without price tags, with flexible prices.

Upmarket shops accept credit cards; many have multilingual staff. Shops open by 9am and close around 7–8pm, even on Sunday. *(See also page 40, Itinerary 5 and page 51, Itinerary 8 for more shopping options.)*

Silk and Tailoring

The most popular shopping item in Vietnam – and particularly Hanoi – is silk. Vietnamese silk is slightly inferior in quality to the Thai version (many shops don't actually sell 100 percent silk) but prices are lower and tailoring is great value. Although off-the-rack clothes are increasingly on sale, most silk shops concentrate on tailoring, using Vietnamese silks and other materials. You can order all types of attire in traditional

or modern designs, in days or even hours. Stick to long-established, reputable outlets. Turnaround capacities vary, but allow time for fittings and alterations, and be very clear about your requirements. Generally, the more you pay, the better the quality.

Recommended shops include **Kenly Silk**, 108 Hang Gai Street and **Khai Silk**, 96 Hang Gai and 121 Nguyen Thai Hoc streets – the latter is Vietnam's most successful silk boutique chain. **Le Vent**, 115 Hang Gai Street, specialises in modern takes on traditional designs in sheer organza; **Cocoon**, 30 Nha Chung Street, sells brightly-coloured taffeta silk with intricate embroidery; and **Que Art Gallery**, 1 Au Trieu Street, sells quality, hand-made silk clothes resembling art works. **Co**, 8 Nha Tho Street, and **Marie Linh**, 1 and 74 Hang Trong Street, are reputable tailors specialising in linens and cottons.

Most shops sell what Hanoi truly excels in – exquisite silk bags and shoes in all shapes, sizes and colours, at amazingly good prices, along with silk ties, scarves and sleeping bags. **Van Phuc** – 11km (6¾ miles) southwest of Hanoi *(see page 59)*, known as 'silk village' – has numerous silk showrooms offering tailoring services. Most accept credit cards and deliver to your hotel. Prices are generally cheaper than Hanoi.

Lacquerware

Hanoi excels in lacquerware – Vietnam's most typical traditional handicraft. Practised

Left: silk products in an array of colours
Right: lacquer trays

for hundreds of years, lacquerware comprises multiple layers of paint mixed with resin applied to a base and polished to a deep, lustrous sheen. Amongst the layers, inlays of mother of pearl, bone, eggshells or designs are added. Countless shops sell lacquerware boxes, bowls, photograph albums, vases and trays, but not all of them made in the traditional method. Mass-produced, synthetic lacquer tat has swamped the market, which can't compare with traditional lacquerware in both durability and charm.

Look out for contemporary lacquerware, handmade but with a more modern style, sometimes with Japanese-influenced shapes and a matt finish. **Minh Tam**, 2 Hang Bong Street, specialises in black and white eggshell lacquerware; and **Innove**, at No 15 Ly Quoc Su Street, sells quality, hand-made lacquerware with contemporary designs.

Ceramics

The best place for ceramics is at the source – **Bat Trang** *(see page 45)*, 15km (9¼ miles) southeast of Hanoi. Bat Trang, specialising for centuries in ceramic production, offers the best choices at competitive prices. Dozens of ceramic outlets sell traditional and contemporary lines; vases, tea sets, mugs, plates, urns, etc, and they can export home for you. In town, many tourist shops sell ceramics, or try **Hang Da Market** (Cho Hang Da) on Duong Thanh Street.

Embroidery

Embroidery – a timeless Vietnamese craft – is another Hanoi speciality. Many shops – especially on Hang Gai Street – sell embroidery and drawn threadwork, although quality varies. **Tan My**, at 66 and 109 Hang Gai Street, and **Chi Vang**, at 17 Trang Tien Street, are reputable outlets selling hand-embroidered work with traditional designs on natural fabrics. **Tuyet Lan**, 10 Ly Quoc Su Street, specialises in children's embroidered items; **Hoa Sua Embroidery and Sewing Shop**, 63 Trang Thi Street, and **Lan Handicrafts**, 28 Au Trieu Street, sell embroidered products made by hearing-impaired children. Many products sold in town are produced in **Quat Dong** – a traditional embroidery village, located some 30km (18¾ miles) south of Hanoi.

Ethnic Minority Goods

Hanoi's proximity to the north's ethnic minority groups is reflected in numerous stores selling ethnic handicrafts and clothes. Each group has their own individual style and colours, with distinctive embroidery and weaving patterns. Unfortunately, goods on the market are increasingly factory-produced tat.

Craftlink, 39 and 43–45 Van Mieu Street, is a non-profit organisation helping ethnic minorities by selling their traditional handicrafts. Also recommended: **Craft Window**, 97 Nguyen Thai Hoc and 58 Hang Be streets,

Above: artist at work in the Old Quarter

Vietnamese Craft Guild, 1a–3–5 To Tich Street, and **Tribal Pan Flute**, 42a Hang Bac Street – who scour remote northern minority villages to buy unusual, traditional ethnic goods and items used in daily life.

GIFTS AND UNUSUAL SOUVENIRS

Buddhist flags/paraphernalia: Hang Quat Street.
Communist party banners/badges: Hang Bong Street, 6 Hang Hom Street.
Communist-style propaganda art posters: 8 Nha Chung and 110 Hang Bac streets.
Conical hats/pith helmets: Hang Gai Street or markets.
Hand-carved wooden objects: Curious Objects, 21 Hang Non Street.
Herbal and traditional teas: kiosks along Hang Dieu Street; Les Comptoirs, 59a Ly Thai To Street; Highway 4, 5 Hang Tre/54 Mai Hac De streets.
Lacquered wooden clogs: Pinocchio, 52 and 122 Hang Bong Street.
Souvenir T-shirts: Hang Gai and Hang Bong streets.
Traditional musical instruments: corner of Hang Non and Hang Manh streets.
Traditional northern liquors: Highway 4.
Wooden seals: Hang Quat Street.
Vietnamese coffee: 79 and 96 Le Van Huu Street.

Homeware and Furnishings

An exciting concept has recently emerged in Vietnam, with the fusion of East meets West, in cuisine, fashion and now high design. Particularly around St Joseph's Cathedral (see page 40), cutting-edge and innovative home decor, giftware and interior design shops combine Asian flair and styles with contemporary Western designs, using traditional local materials such as wood, silk, buffalo horn, lacquer and bamboo. Quality stores include **Mosaique**, No 22, and Italian-run **LaCasa**, No 12, on Nha Tho Street and **Dome**, 71 Hang Trong Street (also 10 Yen The Street and 51 Kim Ma Street).

Objets d'Art and Antiques

Several shops sell antiques and objets d'art, but it's difficult telling the genuine from excellent reproductions. Be aware of customs requirements (see page 90). Recommended for antique and reproduction furniture, objets, curios, statues, fine arts and antiquities are: **Vietnamese House**, 92 Hang Bac Street; **Nguyen Freres**, 3 Phan Chu Trinh and 9 Dinh Tien Hoang streets; **Red Door Deco**, 15 Nha Tho Street; **Indochine House**, 39 Hang Trong Street; **Thuyen Thong**, 63 Nghi Tam Street; and **Duc's Stilt House** (see page 39), off Duong Buoi Street.

Art

Contemporary Vietnamese art has undergone rapid change in the last decade, especially in Hanoi, regarded as Vietnam's artistic centre. With international recognition for Vietnamese art, there has been an explosion of art galleries in Hanoi.

Listed here are the more reputable galleries. **Apricot Gallery**, 40b Hang Bong Street (tel: 04-828 8965, www.apricotartvietnam.com); **Art Vietnam Gallery**, 30 Hang Than Street (tel: 04-927 2349, www.vietnamesefineart.com); **Bui Mai Hien Studio**, 99 Nguyen Thai Hoc Street (tel: 04-846 9614, www.hienkhanhart.com); **Green Palm Gallery**, 110 Hang Gai Street (tel: 04-828 9293, www.greenpalm gallery.com); **Mai Gallery**, 3b Phan Huy Chu Street/183 Hang Bong Street (tel: 04-825 1225/04-828 5854, www.maigalleryvietnam.com); **Salon Natasha**, 30 Hang Bong Street (tel: 04-826 1387, www.artsalonnatasha.com); and the husband and wife team at **Trinh Tuan and Cong Kim Hoa Art Studio**, 17 Ly Quoc Su Street (tel: 04-824 5975, www.tinet.com.vn/tuanhoa).

Right: interior, Duc's Stilt House

EATING OUT

Surprisingly underrated, Vietnamese food is light, subtle in flavour and healthy – and delicious to boot. Dishes – like the country – are diverse, complex and rich in history. Chinese and French occupations contributed major influences, but Vietnamese cuisine is unique in its own right. Herbs, subtly spicy broths, dipping sauces – including a pungent fish sauce (*nuoc mam*) – and condiments are some hallmarks.

Food is boiled, steamed, fried or grilled rather than stir-fried; seafood and fish feature strongly. Like many Asian countries, dining is communal and rice (*com*) is the main staple, eaten together with meat, fish, vegetables and soup dishes. Chopsticks are traditionally used by the Vietnamese. French-style baguette loaves are used for sandwiches. Northern cuisine reflects the colder, seasonally changing weather and Chinese influences; it's less sweet and spicy than the south.

The best place to try authentic, local cuisine is on the street – ranging from pavement stalls, hawkers and basic street kitchens – which Hanoi is famous for. Markets and *bia hoi (see page 84)* also offer good local dishes. Ingredients are bought fresh daily and cooked thoroughly – but stick to clean, busy premises.

Western-style fast food outlets haven't yet taken off – not surprising given that Hanoi has some of the best local 'fast food' in the world – and it's amazingly cheap. Only a decade ago, you'd be hard-pressed to find a decent international, upmarket restaurant. These days, Hanoi is catching up fast with other Asian capitals, with a good range of quality, international-style restaurants and an eclectic global cuisine – influenced by cutting-edge foreign chefs – plus a number of upmarket Vietnamese restaurants, all unbelievably good value for money.

Most street eateries open all day, closing by 8pm – or when food runs out; restaurants generally close 10–11pm. Price categories for a three-course meal for one without drinks are as follows:

$ = under US$10
$$ = US$10–20
$$$ = above US$20

Vietnamese

Cay Cau
De Syloia Hotel, 17A Tran Hung Dao Street
Tel: 04-824 5346
Housed in the boutique De Syloia Hotel, this small restaurant serves excellent Vietnamese cuisine and is very popular with locals. The pomelo salad and pork-stuffed eggplant are highly recommended. Classical music performances in the evenings. $$

Cha Ca La Vong
14 Cha Ca Street
Tel: 04-825 3929
One of Hanoi's most famous dishes, *cha ca* is the only thing served here – fish cooked on a clay brazier at your table – with rice noodles, peanuts and herbs. Overpriced given the no-frills surroundings and simple dish – but the food is delicious and the restaurant an institution, open since 1871. $

Emperor
18b Le Thanh Tong Street
Tel: 04-826 8801
The opulent Emperor is surprisingly informal. Dine in the renovated French villa or open-plan traditional wooden house, with balcony tables above the courtyard. The flavoursome regional Vietnamese cuisine is innovative and exquisitely presented. $$

Above: waitress in ethnic attire at Sofitel Metropole's Spices Garden restaurant

Highway 4 Bar/Restaurant
*5 Hang Tre Street, tel: 04-926 0639, and
54 Mai Hac De Street, tel: 04-976 2647*
Highway 4 specialises in authentic rice wine liquors and North Vietnamese cuisine, particularly steamboat, fish, spring rolls (try the catfish spring rolls with wasabi-based dip) and earthen pot dishes. Amidst traditional northern decor, sit cross-legged at split bamboo low tables – or else ask for a table on the roof terrace. **$**

Le Tonkin
*14 Ngo Van So Street
Tel: 04-943 3457*
Set in a century-old restored French villa, dripping with regional antiquities and ambience. Dine inside or in the garden courtyard. The beautifully presented Vietnamese cuisine is modified to suit Westerners. Evening traditional music performances are an added bonus. Good value for money. **$**

Quan Com Pho
*29 Le Van Huu Street
Tel: 04-943 2356*
Very good value and tasty Vietnamese fare, served in no-frills but bright and clean surroundings. Perfect if you don't like eating on the street. An extensive menu includes regional Vietnamese dishes. **$**

Spices Garden
*Sofitel Metropole, 15 Ngo Quyen Street
Tel: 04-826 6919*
A fabulous hybrid of North Vietnamese cuisine with some creative French influences and flavours, under resident French chef. Lunchtime 'mock' Hanoi street food stalls – served by women in ethnic garb – provide a sanitised introduction to local cuisine. Traditional folk performances on Friday and Saturday nights. **$$**

Wild Rice
*6 Ngo Thi Nham Street
Tel: 04-943 8896*
Visually stunning restaurant incorporating Japanese and minimalist design influences. The contemporary Vietnamese cuisine – reinvented for Western tastes – can vary in standards, but generally is flavoursome, understated and good value. **$$**

Right: courtyard at Emperor restaurant

French

Café des Arts
*11b Bao Khanh Street
Tel: 04-828 7207*
A cosy, lively restaurant straight out of France, with gourmet French regional cuisine, on-going art exhibitions and a flamboyant Parisian host. A la carte favourites include *confit de canard* and steak tartare. **$$**

Hoa Sua Training Restaurant
*28a Ha Hoi Street
Tel: 04-942 4448*
Part of the Hoa Sua project for disadvantaged youth, housed in a beautiful restored villa. Service can be haphazard, but it's for a good cause and the cuisine – French influenced with some Vietnamese – can be surprisingly good. **$**

Le Beaulieu
*Sofitel Metropole, 15 Ngo Quyen Street
Tel: 04-826 6919*
A century on, Le Beaulieu is arguably still the best French restaurant in Vietnam. The award-winning French chef creates innovative and magnificent yet simplistic French cuisine, with the finest local and international ingredients, exquisitely presented. **$$$**

International

Alfresco's
*23L Hai Ba Trung Street
Tel: 04-826 7782*
The place if you crave quality, upmarket fast food. This family-orientated restaurant is popular for its jumbo ribs, imported Australian steaks and burgers, fish and chips, plus decent Mexican dishes, all with generous portions. **$$**

Green Tangerine
48 Hang Be Street
Tel: 04-825 1286
Set in a gorgeous restored French villa in the heart of the Old Quarter. Atmospheric interior, or dine in the garden courtyard. The French chef creates mouthwatering international fusion as well as traditional French with innovative twists. **$$**

KOTO
61 Van Mieu Street
Tel: 04-747 0337
KOTO is a non-profit project providing hospitality training for Hanoi's disadvantaged youth. At this delightful restaurant, trainee staff serve tasty multicultural food: the Mediterranean-style sandwiches and buffet breakfast are recommended. **$**

Restaurant Bobby Chinn
1 Ba Trieu Street
Tel: 04-934 8577
www.bobbychinn.com
Restaurateur and chef Bobby Chinn is an exotic global hybrid, reflected in his fusion Asian-Californian cuisine. This fabulously opulent restaurant features a swish bar, contemporary art and silk drapes. Egyptian *shisha* (water) pipes smoked on scattered silk cushions are optional. **$$**

The Restaurant
Press Club, 59a Ly Thai To Street
Tel: 04-934 0888
Its elegant interior contrasts starkly with the innovative and contemporary Western cuisine, created by its former Australian chef. Light but intensely flavoured dishes break the rules. This, plus cigars, fine wines and discreet dining make this a popular choice for business people. **$$**

Vine Wine Boutique Bar and Café
1a Xuan Dieu Street
Tel: 04-719 8000
Canadian wine enthusiast and chef Donald Berger runs this chic and intimate outfit, deservedly popular for its world-class wines and delicious food. Cuisine is an eclectic mix of global 'comfort foods', including gourmet pizzas and Thai spaghetti. The cellar doubles as an intimate dining room. **$$**

Italian
Luna d'Autunno
11b Dien Bien Phu Street
Tel: 04-823 7338
Italian-run, serving authentic traditional and contemporary Italian cuisine for years. The wood-fired, thin-crust pizzas are regarded as the best in town, but the home-made fresh pastas and risotti are good too, accompanied by fine Italian wines. The garden courtyard is especially charming. **$**

Mediterraneo
23 Nha Tho Street
Tel: 04-826 6288
A good, long established restaurant, run by an Italian couple. Their forte – risotto, home-made pastas (including black *agnolotti*), sausages, cheeses and ice cream. The specials board offers dishes such as Roman-style lamb roast. Book in advance for a balcony table overlooking the cathedral. **$**

Spanish
La Salsa Tapas Bar and Restaurant
25 Nha Tho Street
Tel: 04-828 9052
French-run, but probably the only authentic Spanish tapas bar in Vietnam. Try a selection of tapas, or the excellent southern French and Spanish dishes, including authentic paella, washed down with jugs of sangria or fine wines. The distinctive Spanish ambience draws a sizeable crowd. **$$**

Cafés
Au Lac
57 Ly Thai To Street
Tel: 04-825 7807
Delightful outdoor garden café and bar in a courtyard. An ideal place for a rendezvous, with an extensive drinks list, including decent coffees. The menu features Western and Asian dishes: the inventive salads and goat cheese pizza are recommended. **$**

Highlands Coffee
West Lake: Thanh Nien Street
Hoan Kiem Lake: Kiosk, 38–40 Le Thai To Street; 6th Floor, 38 Le Thai To Street; and 2nd Floor, Ho Guom Plaza, 1–3–5–7 Dinh Tien Hoang Street

Delightful European-style cafés run by Highlands Coffee chain, in prime lakeside locations all over Hanoi. A variety of hot and cold drinks – including sodas and frozen granitas – plus light meals and snacks served all day, including breakfasts, sandwiches, soups and salads. **$**

Little Hanoi
21 Hang Gai Street
Tel: 04-828 8333
A great little café, attractively decked in traditional wood and bamboo, located just north of Hoan Kiem Lake. Serves excellent fresh baguette sandwiches, and light meals such as pastas and soups. **$**

Moca Café
14–16 Nha Tho Street
Tel: 04-825 6334
European-style café near the cathedral; a great place to people watch. Offers an eclectic menu, but best for its fresh-brewed coffees (coffee beans roasted and ground on-site) – try the excellent lattes. The open fireplace is welcome in winter. **$**

Tamarind Café
80 Ma May Street
Tel: 04-926 0580
Imaginative and contemporary vegetarian cuisine, with a strong Asian accent. All-day breakfasts, spring rolls and Asian-style quesadillas are recommended. The fruit juice bar is the best in town. Asian decor reflects the menu: head for the Japanese-style raised wooden platform at the rear. **$**

Hotel Buffets

Great value for money and a chance to enjoy top quality establishments, Hanoi's hotel buffets are well worth sampling – see local magazine listings for current promotions. Recommended: gourmet Sunday brunch at **Le Beaulieu** (Sofitel Metropole) and **Oven D'or Restaurant** (Sheraton Hanoi, K5 Nghi Tam, 11 Xuan Dieu Road, tel: 04-719 9000), and excellent-value buffets throughout the week at **Nikko Hanoi** (84 Tran Nhan Trong Street, tel: 04-822 3535). The 20th-floor **Summit Lounge** (Sofitel Plaza Hanoi, 1 Thanh Nien Road, tel: 04-823 8888) offers sunset buffet barbecues on the terrace.

Street Food

Pho (noodle soup) is considered the north's national dish, synonymous with Hanoi. Eaten anytime, but particularly for breakfast, *pho* is chicken or beef slivers and rice noodles dunked in a hot soup: chilli sauce, limes and fresh herbs are accompaniments. Recommended outlets: **32 and 34 Bat Dan**, **13 Lo Duc**, **63 and 73 Lo Su** streets and particularly **32 Le Van Huu Street**.

Another Hanoi speciality is *bun cha* (barbecued pork patties with herbs and rice noodles) at **1 Hang Manh**, **67 Duong Thanh**, **90 Hang Trong**, **38 and 49 Mai Hac De** and **20 Ta Hien** streets.

Hué speciality *bun bo* is popular in Hanoi (fried beef, noodles and peanuts), best at **67 Hang Dieu Street**. For *banh cuon* (rice pancake filled with minced pork), try **14 Hang Ga Street**. Vietnam's famous spring rolls (*nem*) are more widespread in the south, but try them at Vietnamese restaurants listed here. A good introduction to street food is **Tong Duy Tan Street** (and adjoining **Cam Chi Alley**).

Picnic Food

The following offer cold cuts, cheeses, patés, quiches, sandwiches and salads: **Au Delice**, 19 Han Thuyen Street, tel: 04-972 0548; **Hanoi Gourmet**, 1b Ham Long Street, tel: 04-943 1009; **Le Beaulieu Gourmand**, 56 Ly Thai To Street, tel: 04-821 8702; **Press Club Deli**, 59a Ly Thai To Street, tel: 04-934 0888; **The Deli**, 6 Tong Dan Street, tel: 04-934 2335; and **Vine Wine Boutique Bar and Café** *(see pages 82/83)*. **Little Hanoi** *(see this page)* and **No Noodles**, 20 Nha Chung Street, tel: 04-928-5969, do excellent takeaway sandwiches.

Right: Vietnamese-style *pho* noodles

NIGHTLIFE

Hanoians are not known for their partying; 'R and R' could stand for 'rise and retire early' and streets are generally dark and deserted after 11pm. For a capital city, Hanoi's nightlife is low-key and limited, particularly nightclubs; but given the city's ideology, this is hardly surprising. Early closing hours don't help – courtesy of government restrictions and fluctuating midnight curfews.

However, the nightlife has improved substantially in the last few years, and although Hanoi appears sleepy after dark, there are some great bars, many with a friendly, pub-like ambience and an emerging live music scene. Quite a few top-end international hotels and restaurants have stylish in-house bars. If you want to be like a local, try the *bia hoi* – local fresh beer outlets – a relative newcomer on the scene introduced by the Czechs, but now a social institution. An alternative option is traditional cultural performances, making for an interesting (and inexpensive) night out.

Bars

The last few years have seen several new bars open, the majority located around the centre. Closing times vary for street bars, as it depends on sporadic police raids, but some bars manage to stay open until the early hours. Practically all run happy hours, usually from 5pm onwards.

Funky Monkey
15b Hang Hanh Street
Tel: 04-928 6113
One of the coolest bars in town, frequented by a predominantly young Vietnamese and foreign crowd. Loud and hip music, resident DJs, funky decor and pool table.

Highway 4 Bar/Restaurant
5 Hang Tre Street, tel: 04-926 0639, and
54 Mai Hac De Street, tel: 04-976 2647
Highway 4 brews its own traditional northern medicinal liquors and stocks minority varieties, including exotic 'gecko' and 'black bees' potions. These, plus traditional decor and authentic North Vietnamese cuisine, create a unique bar experience.

JJ's Sports Bar
Hilton Hanoi Opera, 1 Le Thanh Tong Street
Tel: 04-933 0500
This lounge-style sports bar is one of the best places to watch sports and entertainment events, screened daily on three screens. Darts and pool are also available. Prices reflect the five-star premises.

Le Club Bar
Sofitel Metropole Hanoi, 56 Ly Thai To Street
Tel: 04-826 6919
Oozes colonial charm with whirring ceiling fans, wooden floors and rattan chairs. Lovely any time of day; with a well-stocked bar and resident pianist. The more informal al fresco **Bamboo Bar** shares the same services.

Ly Club
51 Ly Thai To Street
Tel: 04-936 3069
Housed in an old villa, this gorgeous club-style lounge recreates an Indochina ambience with stunning décor. Serves a light Asian and Western menu, afternoon teas, plus fine wines and spirits. A mini-theatre downstairs hosts evening performances of traditional performing arts.

Polite Pub
5 Bao Khanh Street
Tel: 04-825 0959

Above: hip Funky Monkey bar

One of Hanoi's longest-running bars and popular with both expats and tourists of all ages. This dimly-lit bar screens major sporting fixtures and offers good music, pub grub, cheap drinks, plus a snooker room and a pool table.

R and R Tavern

47 Lo Su Street
Tel: 04-934 4109
Long-established bar, run by a laid-back American. Especially popular with returning US war veterans, and boasts an impressive CD collection. Local rock bands perform at weekends. Bar food includes a selection of Tex Mex dishes.

Restaurant Bobby Chinn

1 Ba Trieu Street
Tel: 04-934 8577
Open-plan bar in well-known fusion Asian-Californian restaurant. Stunning decor and one of the classiest, best-stocked bars in town, with over 100 cocktails and an eclectic selection of fine wines. Disabled friendly.

Summit Lounge

Sofitel Plaza Hanoi, 1 Thanh Nien Road
Tel: 04-823 8888
All-glass bar and outside terrace on the 20th floor offers the best city views. Sunset barbecues are hosted daily in warmer weather. Low-key bands perform nightly.

Terrace Bar

Press Club, 59a Ly Thai To Street
Tel: 04-934 0888
Located on the Press Club's third floor, a pleasant, upmarket and open-terrace bar, perfect for al fresco drinking. Busiest on Friday nights, when expatriates let off steam with themed party nights or music from international DJ's.

Vine Wine Boutique Bar and Café

1a Xuan Dieu Road
Tel: 04-719 8000
Stocks a huge selection of fine wines (not found elsewhere in Hanoi) displayed on signature wall racks. This internationally managed, small but glamorous bar is host to an eclectic mix of clientele. Adjoining restaurant serves equally eclectic food.

Right: Bobby Chinn's plush interior

Bia Hoi

You'll find countless *bia hoi* all over Hanoi, where local males congregate to drink dirt-cheap and freshly brewed draught beer. These places are a great way to meet Hanoians. Most are pretty basic with their miniature plastic stools spilling out onto pavements, but they serve good-value food to soak up the beer. Drinking starts as early as 6am; as the beer has a 24-hour shelf life, most close by 10pm – or when the beer runs out.

Recommended *bia hoi*: **Ta Hien and Luong Ngoc Quyen junction, 24 Tong Dan Street, 55 and 72 Ma May Street, Chan Cam and Ly Quoc Su junction, 19C Ngoc Ha Street, 34a Phan Vhu Trinh Street** and **124 Hai Ba Trung Street** – the latter more upscale, serving *bia tuoi* (pressurized beer). Look out also for reliable *bia hoi* chains, **Bia Anchor** and **Hai Xom**.

Clubs

There are just a few clubs in Hanoi aimed at the international market (Hanoi isn't the place for clubbing). Although Hanoi lags far behind Ho Chi Minh City in terms of quality and quantity, the club scene is starting to improve, particularly those aimed at Vietnamese youth.

Apocalypse Now

2 Dong Tac Street, Dong Da District
One of Hanoi's longest running and popular nightclubs has relocated to brand new premises. With its trademark DJ stand, pool table and pumping dance floor, this is a sanitised and blander version of the former Apocalypse, but still worth a shot. A fair way out from the centre.

Jazz Club by Quyen Van Minh
31 Luong Van Can Street
Tel: 04-828 7890
The first jazz club in Vietnam, founded by the godfather of Vietnamese jazz, Quyen Van Minh, who plays the saxophone along with an ensemble that sometimes includes visiting international performers. Daily performances start after 8.30pm.

New Century
10 Trang Thi Street
Tel: 04-928 5286
Hanoi gets hip here, with lasers, high-tech equipment and the latest sounds. Popular with young Vietnamese and foreigners, this nightclub has a huge dance floor and several bars. Packed on Saturdays and Sundays, it generally stays open till late. Shame about the surly 'security guards'.

Cultural Performances

Hanoi's **Opera House** (1 Trang Tien Street, tel: 04-933 0113) is a stunning, century-old venue, with excellent technical equipment, hosting occasional ballet, theatre and orchestral, and choral and opera performances, sometimes with international artists.

Vietnamese traditional theatre has strong Chinese influences and integrates music, singing, dance and mime, with plots, songs and characters familiar to local audiences. Vietnam's oldest surviving stage art, *hat cheo* ('popular theatre') originates and is performed exclusively in the north. Anti-establishment and with peasant origins, *hat cheo* often presents popular legends and everyday events, with biting satire. **Hanoi Cheo Theatre** (15 Nguyen Dinh Chieu Street, tel: 04-943 4205) hosts performances thrice weekly.

Cai luong ('modern theatre') originated in South Vietnam in the early 20th century, but has gained popularity in the north. This incorporates Western staging techniques and contemporary themes. **Golden Bell Theatre** (72 Hang Bac Street, tel: 04-825 7823) hosts traditional *cai luong* on a weekly basis.

Introduced from China in the 13th century, *hat tuong* ('classical theatre') evolved from Chinese opera but is Vietnamese in style. Formalistic, it employs gestures and scenery similar to Chinese theatre. **Hong Ha Theatre** (51a Duong Thanh Street, tel: 04-825 2803) hosts occasional *tuong* performances – as well as *hat cheo*, *cai luong* and modern drama. For the above venues, check local press or outside the respective venues for details of performances. **Ly Club** (51 Ly Thai To Street, tel: 04-936 3069) stages, several times a week, traditional performing arts such as *cheo*, *ca tru*, *tuong* and Hue court music (*nha nhac*) in a purpose-built mini theatre.

Traditional water puppetry shows – unique to the Red River Delta – are performed thrice nightly (5.15pm, 6.30pm and 8pm) and on Sundays (9.30am) at the **Thang Long Water Puppet Theatre** (57b Dinh Tien Hoang Street, tel: 04-825 5450).

Above: the stunning Hanoi Opera House

CALENDAR OF EVENTS

Celebrations in Vietnam are either new and Communist-fixed public holidays, or traditional and religious festivals. With the latter, exact dates vary each year as they follow the lunar calendar, which starts with Tet, the Lunar New Year. By counting the days from a new moon, it is possible to calculate where dates in the lunar month fall on the Gregorian calendar. Alternatively, consult a Vietnamese calendar, which gives both systems.

January–February

Tet (1st–7th day of 1st lunar month): The biggest, most important celebration of the year, **Tet Nguyen Dan** (in full) heralds the start of the Vietnamese Lunar New Year. *Tet* ('festival') falls between late January and mid-February. Officially, the public holiday falls on the first three days of the new year; in reality, the city shuts down for the week. Many Hanoi workers return to the countryside and overseas Vietnamese rush home for family reunions and holidays.

Perfume Pagoda Festival (Chua Huong; starts 6th day of the 1st lunar month): Thousands of Buddhist pilgrims flock to one of Vietnam's most revered pilgrimage sites, southwest of Hanoi, to pray for good luck in the coming year. The festival lasts until the middle of the third lunar month.

March–April

Liberation Day (30 April): A national holiday, marking South Vietnam's surrender to the North Vietnamese army in 1975.

Thay Pagoda Festival (5th–7th day of the 3rd lunar month): In celebration of the pagoda's revered Buddhist monk and puppeteer, festivities include traditional water puppetry and rowing contests.

Le Mat Festival (23rd day of the 3rd lunar month): Snake Village celebrates a local legend, with three poisonous snake dishes, snake dances and snake-beheading act.

May–June

International Labour Day (1 May): This national holiday falls back-to-back with Liberation Day (30 April) – a two-day break.

Ho Chi Minh's Birthday (19 May): Parades with streets and buildings festooned

with flags, celebrating the birth of the founder of modern-day Vietnam.

Phat Dan (Buddha's birth, enlightenment and death; 8th day of the 4th lunar month): Buddha's rites of passage are celebrated in pagodas, temples and homes.

Tet Duan Ngo (Summer Solstice Day; 5th day of the 5th lunar month): Festivities to ensure good health and well-being: offerings are made to spirits, ghosts and the God of Death to ward off summer epidemics.

July–August

Trang Nguyen (Wandering Souls Day; 15th day of the 7th lunar month): The second most important Vietnamese festival. Graves are cleaned and offerings are made in homes and pagodas for the wandering souls of the forgotten dead.

September–October

Tet Trung Thu (Mid-Autumn/Moon Festival; 15th day of the 8th lunar month): A children's festival. In addition to dragon dances, a children's parade with candle-lit lanterns accompanied by drums and cymbals takes place. In the lead-up, streets in the Old Quarter heave with lanterns and 'moon cakes' filled with a sweet bean paste.

National Day (2 September): A national holiday commemorating the Declaration of Independence in 1945, which founded the Democratic Republic of Vietnam.

November–December

Christmas (25 December): Celebrated by Vietnamese and expat Christians. Midnight Mass and Christmas Day services are held in churches across the north. On Christmas Eve night, central Hanoi comes to a virtual standstill, with everyone out on the streets.

Right: celebrating Liberation Day

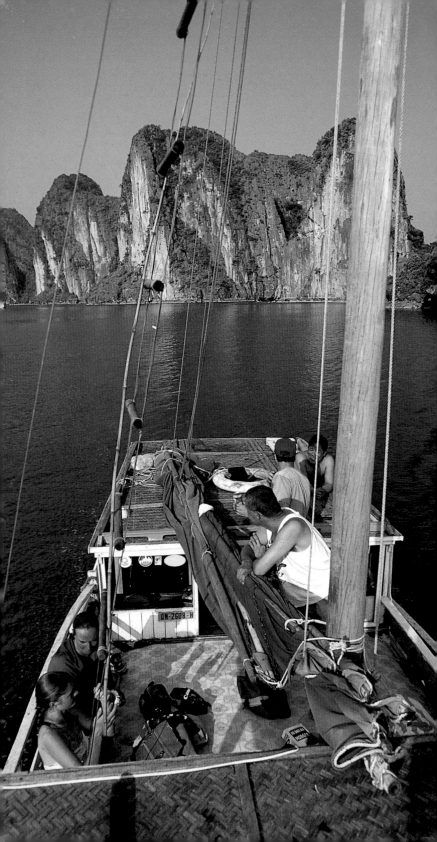

Practical Information

GETTING THERE

By Air

Hanoi is amply served by direct flights operated by many Asian airlines. Others – such as American Airlines, British Airways, Cathay Pacific, Continental, KLM, Lufthansa, SAS, Qantas and United Airlines – fly into Hanoi under a code share agreement with Vietnam Airlines, the national carrier.

Getting to the City

Hanoi's **Noi Bai International Airport** is 35km (21 miles) north of Hanoi, about 45 minutes by road. Outside the arrival hall is a designated taxi rank. Official metered taxis to the city cost US$10. Insist that your taxi take you straight to your hotel; some may take you elsewhere for a cut in commission. Do not use unlicensed taxicabs.

Airport minibuses depart directly for the city; tickets cost US$2, terminating at 2 Quang Trung Street. Air-conditioned buses (No 7) also depart for the city; tickets cost 2500d, but the journey takes around two hours.

International departure tax from Hanoi is US$14. For **flight information**, tel: (04) 886 5318/886 6527.

By Rail and Road

It is possible to enter North Vietnam from southern China via three entry points: by road or rail via Lao Cai in the northwest and Dong Da (near Lang Son) in the northeast, and by road at Mong Cai, in the northeast.

TRAVEL ESSENTIALS

Climate/When to Visit

Hanoi and the north have four distinct seasons, although weather patterns vary annually. Broadly speaking, winter lasts from December to March: dry, cold air sweeps in from China contributing to temperatures averaging 10–15°C (50–59°F), before starting to climb in March, averaging 20°C (68°F). February and March can be damp with drizzle and overcast skies. The northern mountains experience cooler temperatures, sometimes frost or snow during winter. Spring lasts from March to April and can be quite pleasant; May to September brings unsettled weather and high temperatures, averaging 30–36°C (86–97°F). Summer sees most rainfall, coinciding with the typhoon season, which peaks around August. Humidity climbs to uncomfortable and sticky levels (around 90 percent in July), although it's lower in the mountains. Autumn – late September to early December – is the loveliest time to visit: humidity levels drop, with blue skies, little rain and pleasant temperatures of 25–30°C (77–86°F).

Tet, the Vietnamese Lunar New Year (*see page 87*), falls in January or February. On either side of Tet, transport into and out of Hanoi is booked up with local and overseas Vietnamese returning home. During Tet, Hanoi virtually shuts down: many businesses and restaurants close for at least three days – sometimes the entire week – (in the lead-up, some businesses come to a grinding halt) and travel may be difficult. There shouldn't be any problem booking hotels in Hanoi, although some run on a skeleton service.

Left: picturesque Halong Bay
Right: train travel offers a chance to mix with the locals

Visas

With a few exceptions (ASEAN– Association of Southeast Asian Nations – nationals for instance), you need a visa to enter Vietnam; single-entry tourist visas are valid for 30 days and cost around US$65. Some embassies issue visas for three months and multiple-entry visas. Apply through a travel agent, or direct with a Vietnamese embassy or consulate (for a list of Vietnamese foreign missions overseas, check www.mofa.gov.vn).

Visas begin on the date specified, not the date you enter Vietnam. Certain tour operators in Vietnam now issue visas on arrival (*see page 100 – tour operators)*: visas are issued upon presentation of a pre-arranged confirmation letter at a 'visa on arrival' desk at Hanoi's airport. Visas can be extended locally (usually 30 days), although subject to the mood of the government – arrange this through a tour company.

Vaccinations/Health

The most important vaccinations are hepatitis A and typhoid fever. The incidence of Hepatitis B in Vietnam is high and tetanus remains a concern. In high-risk areas, or off the beaten track, shots for Japanese encephalitis is recommended. Rabies is an increasing problem: vaccinations should be considered. Measles and polio boosters should be up-to-date. Malaria risk is generally low in Vietnam; for Hanoi, malarial prevention is not advised. However, for travel in rural areas, seek medical advice regarding malarial prevention, sleep under a mosquito net, use DEET repellant and be sure to cover up from dusk to dawn.

Customs

On arrival, you must fill in a landing card; a yellow duplicate copy is given to you. On your departure, hand this back to airport customs officials; don't lose it, otherwise you may be fined. This form, together with your passport, will be requested for police registration when checking in at hotels (*see page 97 – Police).*

To protect Vietnamese heritage, it is illegal to export Vietnamese antiques (anything prior to 1945), or items deemed of 'cultural and historical significance' without permission from the Ministry of Culture. Buy such items through a reputable outlet that arranges the necessary export license and paperwork, even for reproductions. Without this paperwork, you could be fined or have your suspected items seized. Video cameras and tapes, film, DVDs, CDs, cameras, electronic items and reading materials can fall under scrutiny when arriving and departing Vietnam.

Electricity

Vietnam's voltage is 220 volts (50Hz), sometimes 110 volts in rural areas. In the north, electric sockets are two pin, round prongs: bring adapter plugs. As the electrical current varies, use a surge protector when running sensitive electronic equipment. Hanoi is prone to power cuts, especially in the summer. Older buildings may have faulty (and dangerous) electrical wiring and sockets.

Time Difference

Vietnam is 7 hours ahead of Greenwich Mean Time (GMT).

GETTING ACQUAINTED

Geography

Hanoi covers 921sq km (355sq miles) and is located in the Red River Delta (15,000sq km; 5,791sq miles) in the centre of North Vietnam. Laos lies to the west, China to the north and northeast.

Government and Economy

Vietnam is a Socialist Republic ruled by the Vietnamese Communist Party from the capital, Hanoi. Vietnam has a single-party system, with its political institutions borrowed from Soviet and Chinese models. Political control lies firmly in the hands of the Communists and opposition parties are prohibited. There are no free elections and any criticism of the Communist Party or government is forbidden.

Since the mid-1980s, *doi moi* ('renovation') has brought market-based economic reforms, and the economy has developed and improved – aided by the US lifting its trade embargo and a 2001 US bilateral trade agreement, plus Vietnam joining ASEAN. But in the north particularly, the economy has never reached its potential, especially with foreign investment and tourism. Vietnam is essentially an agrarian country, and it is ranked 109 out of 175 countries on the Human Development Index.

Religion

The main religious and philosophical influences in Vietnam are Buddhism, Taoism and Confucianism, mixed with ancestor and spirit worship. China has been the greatest influence: Mahayana Buddhism is the predominant religion. There are around 600 pagodas and temples in and around Hanoi. Pagodas (*chua*) worship Buddha, while temples (*den*) have Taoist and Confucian elements, dedicated to other gods, national heroes or guardian spirits. Communal houses (*dinh*) are for community use and honour heroes and founding patrons. Catholics constitute around 8–10 percent of the population.

Population

Vietnam is the world's 14th most populous country, with 54 ethnic groups – more than any other Asian country. Indigenous Viet (or *Kinh*), account for 87 percent of Vietnam's 81 million population. Most of the 5.5 million ethnic minorities live in the northern mountainous regions. Hanoi's population is around three million, the second largest metropolis, behind Ho Chi Minh City in the south.

How Not to Offend

Vietnam is a developing country, with piles of red tape, sometimes atrocious service (the latter an alien concept to most Vietnamese) and things don't always going to plan. But being aggressive, argumentative or angry will get you nowhere: you just end up 'losing face' and achieving nothing. Remain respectful, polite and smile a lot. Confucian attitudes remain strong and seniority demands respect.

Although the young increasingly wear Westernised attire, as a visitor you should dress modestly – especially women and in pagodas and temples and ethnic minority areas. The Vietnamese admire neatness and cleanliness. Before entering private homes and religious sites, take your shoes off. Ask permission before taking photographs, especially with the ethnic minorities. Nudity and

topless sunbathing is an absolute no-no. Any disrespect to the founder Ho Chi Minh is viewed as very offensive, even punishable.

MONEY MATTERS

Currency

The Vietnamese currency is the dong (VND or d); in 200, 500, 1,000, 2,000, 5,000, 10,000, 20,000, 50,000, 100,000 and 500,000 note denominations. Take care with 5,000d and 20,000d notes – they are the same size and colour (blue). Coins – 200d, 500d, 1,000d, 2,000d and 5,000d – are being re-introduced into circulation.

A dual-currency system means that transactions can be made in US dollars – widely accepted and quoted in tourist hotels, restaurants, tour operators and shops. The dong's value against the dollar hovers at over 15,000d.

When exchanging money and receiving change in either US dollars or dong, check your change and for torn, faded or crumpled notes, as these may be refused. Dong is non-convertible and not available outside Vietnam. You cannot legally bring in or take out dong as a foreigner, so change spare dong into US dollars before departing. When exchanging dong to US dollars, an exchange certificate, ATM receipt – even travel documents – may be required as proof of where this was obtained: always keep your ATM and exchange receipts.

Credit Cards

Payments by major credit cards – especially Visa and MasterCard – are becoming more widely accepted in high-end establishments. Cash advances can be made against them at major banks and some authorised exchange booths at hotels and tour companies.

Right: credit card payment is accepted in many places

Exchanging Money

Buy traveller's cheques in US dollars. Most banks have currency exchanges: outside banking hours, use authorised currency exchanges at hotels and tour companies. You can also exchange money at gold shops, which generally give favourable rates. Do not change money on the street (money-changers hover around the GPO and Hoan Kiem Lake); there is a chance of being ripped off, and you may need official receipts to change dong back into other currencies.

Banks

ANZ: 14 Le Thai To Street, tel: 04-825 8190 (open through lunch); **Citibank**: 17 Ngo Quyen Street, tel: 04-825 1950; **Sacombank**: 87 Hang Bac Street, tel: 04-926 1392; (Mon–Fri, 8am–8pm; Sat 8am–5pm, Sun 8am–4pm); **Vietcombank**: 198 Tran Quang Khai Street, 2 Hang Bai Street, 108 Cau Go Street and 120 Hang Trong Street, (24-hour hotline, tel: 04-824 5716).

ATMs

ATMs dispense dong, not dollars. ANZ, Sacombank and Vietcombank have 24-hour ATMs that accept Visa and MasterCard. ATMs at ANZ and Sacombank also accept Cirrus, JCB and Plus cards.

Tipping

Tipping is not part of the culture, but always appreciated. Upmarket hotels and restaurants include a 5 percent service charge on bills. Around 5–10 percent should suffice as a tip for good service; avoid excessive amounts.

Price Differences

Vietnam operates a dual-price system for some goods and services, with a higher price for foreigners. The government is slowly phasing this system out: trains and airlines now operate a single price system, but some tourist attractions, hotels, buses and services still retain dual-pricing. In many places – such as at markets and shops with unpriced goods – foreigners will always be quoted higher prices.

GETTING AROUND

Taxis

Hiring a metered taxi is a relatively cheap way of getting around Hanoi; a short ride in town is roughly around 11,000–15,000d. Unfortunately, there are cowboy operators. Scams include taking the longest route possible (some streets are one-way, but this is abused further), driving as slowly as possible and operating bogus meters that spin suspiciously fast. Always get your hotel reception to call a taxi, or find a taxi outside five-star hotels (these are reliable and many drivers speak English). Failing that, **Hanoi Taxi** (tel: 04-853 5353), **CP Taxi** (tel: 04-824 1999) and **Mai Linh Taxi** (tel: 04-822 2666) are usually reliable; always ask for the meter to be switched on. If hiring a taxi for itineraries and excursions; arrange this through your hotel. Taxis to the airport (US$10 flat rate) congregate outside the Vietnam Airlines office at 2 Quang Trung Street, or tel: 04-934 4070/04-873 3333.

Motorbikes

Motorbikes are the principal form of transport in Hanoi and they can cause mayhem – so you need to keep a constant lookout when crossing the roads.

Motorbike taxis (*xe om*), found on street corners, are the fastest way to get around. Negotiate the fare first: around 5,000–8,000d for short trips, or 1,000d per kilometre. Take care using *xe om* after dark (especially women) and hold on tight to your possessions – there have been several incidences of bag snatching. Always wear a helmet.

Motorbikes are a great way of experiencing the countryside, but with the appalling road sense, take extreme care. Motorbikes can be rented from travellers' cafés and rental shops in the Old Quarter; try

Left: motorbikes are a quick way of getting around

Hang Bac Street or **Cuong's Motorbike Adventure**, 1 Luong Ngoc Quyen Street (tel: 04-926 1534); around US$5–10 per day. You'll need an international driver's license. Traffic accidents are the single largest health concern in Vietnam: always wear a helmet (a legal requirement on major highways) and make sure you are adequately insured. You can buy international-standard helmets from **Protec**, 3 Dang Thai Than Street. Several tour companies run motorbike tours in the north (*see page 100 – tour operators*).

Bicycles

With Hanoi's increasing motorised traffic, cycling is not the romantic (and safe) option it once was. However, it's still a good way to get around, but wear a helmet. Bicycles can be hired for under US$1 a day; try outlets along Hang Bac Street, hotels or tour companies. **Buffalo Tours** rent out mountain bikes; some tour operators run mountain biking trips (*see page 100 – tour operators*).

Car Hire

Car hire is ideal for excursions outside Hanoi. Self-drive for tourists and short-term visitors is not an option and strongly discouraged (a blessing in disguise). Cars come with drivers: always hire a car from reputable tour operators (*see page 100*). Prices vary from US$30–70 a day (inclusive of petrol, parking and drivers fees). Drivers don't usually speak English, so you may need to hire a guide (US$10–35 a day) in addition.

Buses

Hanoi's recently expanded city bus fleet is clean and modern, with new bus shelters, clear route signs and bus lanes. Heavily subsidised tickets cost a 2,500d flat rate. Although city buses make frequent stops along easy-to-follow routes, language difficulties may cause problems and at peak times buses are packed to capacity.

Cyclos

Cyclos (*xich lo*) – three-wheel bicycle rickshaws – are found in the Old Quarter, outside hotels and main tourist outlets. Cyclos offer close-up views of Hanoi's streets, are environmentally friendly and double as local guides. They are, however, banned from certain streets, and, in a government attempt to regulate unscrupulous operators, numbers are dwindling. As a general guide, pay US$1.50–2 per hour, or around 8,000–10,000d, for a short hop in the city centre. Misunderstandings with cyclos stem mostly from miscommunication, although some will invarably try to overcharge.

Wherever possible, hire a cyclo through your hotel, or outside high-end hotels, especially for tours. Hotel staff can set a price for you and explain exactly where you want to go (bring a map). Arrange the price beforehand and carry small denominations for the exact fare. Do not use cyclos after dark – especially if you are solo and female. At any time, hold on to your possessions.

HOURS AND HOLIDAYS

Business hours

Most banks, public services and state-run offices work Monday to Friday, from 7.30–8.30am, closing between 4–5pm; some offices work Saturday. From 11.30am–1.30pm, most places shut for lunch and a siesta; this includes main banks. Museums roughly follow the same hours, but generally close on Monday (sometimes Fridays) and some remain open at lunch. Tourist-orientated shops work seven-day weeks, open by 9am and close between 7–9pm. Markets open early, winding down by late afternoon. Pagodas and temples open until the evening.

Official Public Holidays

New Year's Day: 1 January
Tet: January/February
Liberation Day: 30 April
International Labour Day: 1 May
National Day/Independence Day:
2 September

ACCOMMODATION

Hanoi still has a long way to go compared to standards of service and accommodation found in other Asian capitals. Some older hotels badly need refurbishing and still offer Communist-style service. However, this has greatly improved in the last few years, with the opening of several new five-star hotels and more mini-hotels (privately-run, budget hotels) – but is still woefully limited in mid-range choices. The hotel oversupply means it's generally not difficult reserving accommodation, even in peak times. Although room rates work out higher than other developing countries, big discounts are always possible even in top-end hotels, with promotions, off-season rates and reservations via the Internet and travel agents.

Many hotels are unfortunately located along noisy streets: double-glazed windows help, or ask for a room at the rear for some peace. Rates are subject to 10 percent government tax and 5 percent service charge. Price categories below are starting rates for a standard double room:

$ = under US$50
$$ = US$50–100
$$$ = US$100–150
$$$$ = above US$150
** = disabled friendly

$$$$
Hanoi Daewoo Hotel
360 Kim Ma Street
Tel: 04-831 5000; Fax: 04-831 5010
www.hanoi-daewoohotel.com
This five-star luxury hotel is located west of the city centre. Occupies an immense complex with offices and an apartment block. It has an excellent fitness centre, landscaped swimming pool, eight food and beverage outlets, ballroom facilities, plus a huge collection of contemporary Vietnamese art on display.

Hilton Hanoi Opera
1 Le Thanh Tong Street
Tel: 04-933 0500; Fax: 04-933 0530
www.hanoi.hilton.com
Relatively new, mock colonial-style hotel, mirroring the adjacent Opera House. Located in central Hanoi, the five-star Hilton is good value and has three restaurants, sports bar, outdoor swimming pool and convention facilities. Its 269 rooms offer excellent bathrooms, with large separate shower unit. **

Hanoi Horison Hotel
40 Cat Linh Street
Tel: 04-733 0808; Fax: 04-733 0888
www.swiss-belhotel.com

Owned by Swiss-belhotel, this five-star hotel lies on a noisy, nondescript road west of the centre. However, luxury facilities include health club, tennis courts and swimming pool, plus 250 comfortable, attractive rooms. Excellent corporate facilities include ballroom and office floors. **

Melia Hanoi
44b Ly Thuong Kiet Street
Tel: 04-934 3343; Fax: 04-934 3344
www.meliahanoi.com
One of Hanoi's newest glitzy high-rise hotels, the Spanish-managed Melia is located in the French Quarter. This five-star is geared towards the executive traveller, with 306 deluxe rooms, outstanding business and conference facilities, Vietnam's largest ballroom and rooftop helipad. **

Hotel Nikko Hanoi
84 Tran Nhan Tong Street
Tel: 04-822 3535; Fax: 04-822 3555
www.hotelnikkohanoi.com.vn
The joint-Japanese owned five-star hotel – a favourite with Japanese and Asian guests – overlooks Reunification Park, southwest of the centre. The 260 spacious rooms have minimalist decor and excellent bathrooms; top floors afford good city views. Benkay is regarded as one of Vietnam's premier Japanese restaurants. **

Sheraton Hanoi Hotel
K5, Nghi Tam, 11 Xuan Dieu Road
Tel: 04-719 9000; Fax: 04-719 9001
www.sheraton.com
Hanoi's newest five-star, the Sheraton lies in landscaped gardens on West Lake. Facilities include lakeside swimming pool, floodlit tennis courts, conference facilities, function rooms and bars and restaurants. Well-appointed rooms have spacious bathrooms with separate shower and lake views.

Sofitel Metropole Hanoi
15 Ngo Quyen Street
Tel: 04-826 6919; Fax: 04-826 6920
www.sofitel-Hanoi-Vietnam.com
Charming century-old hotel located in the city centre and French Quarter. The former Grand Hotel Metropole Palace is steeped in history, and boasts an impressive guest list:

Right: courtyard at the Moon River Retreat

Noel Coward, Charlie Chaplin and Jane Fonda are some of the luminaries who have stayed here. Major renovations have vastly improved its creature comforts. The Old Wing rooms are small and quaint, while the newer Opera Wing rooms remain faithful to the colonial style. Facilities include swimming pool, Clark Hatch fitness centre, three bars and two excellent restaurants.

Sofitel Plaza Hanoi
1 Thanh Nien Road
Tel: 04-823 8888; Fax: 04-829 3888
www.accorhotels.com/asia
The five-star Plaza's striking stepped architecture dominates Hanoi's skyline, located on West Lake. The 322 light, comfortable rooms offer deluxe bathroom fixtures and huge glass windows, with commanding lake and river views. Popular with tourists and corporate travellers; of note are the Club Floors, all-weather swimming pool with retractable roof and all-glass 20th-floor bar.

$$
Army Hotel
33c Pham Ngu Lao Street
Tel: 04-825 2896; Fax: 04-825 9276
e-mail: armyhotel@fpt.vn
Run by the army, but don't let that put you off. This pleasant, low-rise hotel is situated in quiet, leafy grounds in the French Quarter's east. Recently refurbished (although still endearingly old-fashioned), 82 rooms surround a saltwater swimming pool; plus conference hall and fitness centre. **

De Syloia Hotel
17a Tran Hung Dao Street
Tel: 04-824 5346; Fax: 04-824 1083
www.desyloia.com
Small, friendly boutique hotel, popular with corporate travellers and tourists, located in the French Quarter's south. Excellent in-house Vietnamese restaurant, plus business centre and health club. The 33 rooms are cosy and comfortable.

Moon River Retreat
Bac Cau 3, Ngoc Thuy Village
Long Bien District
Tel: 04-943 8896; Fax: 04-943 6299
e-mail: wildrice@fpt.vn
New luxury riverside retreat in a tranquil village setting, 5km (3 miles) from central Hanoi. Features traditional Asian architecture in tropical gardens, with comfortable en-suite guestrooms and fine-dining restaurant in authentic timber houses, plus terraced bar. Organises a range of traditional activities, including cooking classes.

Sunway Hotel Hanoi
19 Pham Dinh Ho Street
Tel: 04-971 3888; Fax: 04-971 3555
www.sunwayhanoi.com
Relatively new four-star, award-winning boutique hotel, located south of the centre on a leafy street. Facilities include a jazz bar, excellent Allante restaurant and business centre. The 143 well-appointed rooms have triple glazed windows to keep out the noise, with an 'all-in-one service' button.

$
Anh Dao Hotel
37 Ma May Street
Tel: 04-826 7151; Fax: 04-828 2008
www.camellia-hotels.com
Popular mini-hotel located on the atmospheric (but noisy) Old Quarter street. One of the better 'budget' options with good service, although in need of refurbishment and has no lift. Larger rooms have balconies. Rates include Internet use and breakfast.

Sunshine Hotel
42 Ma May Street
Tel: 04-926 1559; Fax: 04-926 1558
www.sinhcafetour.com
New friendly mini-hotel in the heart of the Old Quarter. The 15 rooms are spotless, with bathtub, air-con, fridge and satellite TV, plus breakfast thrown in. Higher prices afford larger rooms with balcony at front, although these suffer from noise. There is no lift.

Win Hotel
34 Hang Hanh Street
Tel: 04-828 7371; Fax: 04-824 7448
e-mail: winhotel@yahoo.com
Central location in the Old Quarter, on a leafy café strip. This small, popular and friendly mini-hotel has 10 spacious rooms, with traditional dark wood decor. Front rooms have balconies and bathtubs, although may be noisy; there is no lift.

Serviced Apartments

$$$
Somerset Grand Hanoi
49 Hai Ba Trung Street
Tel: 04-934 2342; Fax: 04-934 2343
www.the-ascott.com
One- to three-bedroom spacious and homely apartments, located in the French Quarter, with monthly and daily rates. The 185 fully serviced, furnished apartments have well-equipped kitchens and access to in-house leisure, business and shopping facilities. Somerset's second property at West Lake has apartments which are more family-orientated.

$$
Sofitel Serviced Apartments
1 Thanh Nien Road
Tel: 04-823 8888; Fax: 04-829 3888

www.sofitelapartments.com
Opened in 2003 and located in the Sofitel Plaza, the 36 luxury, ultra-modern one- and two-bedroom apartments are fully furnished in contemporary Asian style and feature well-equipped, self-contained kitchens. Weekly and monthly rates include full services and hotel facilities.

$
Chesterton Apartments
4 Pham Su Manh Street
Tel: 04-934 6000; Fax: 04-934 5949
e-mail: hanh@chesterton.com.vn
Good location in the French Quarter and exceptionally good value. Four furnished, one-bedroom apartments and a studio, tastefully decorated and housed in a colonial-style villa. Daily rates (long-term rates negotiable) include housekeeping.

HEALTH & EMERGENCIES

Hygiene/General Health

Don't drink from the tap; drink plenty of purified or sealed bottled water to stay hydrated. Only consume ice in upmarket establishments. Meat and fish should be thoroughly cooked, while pre-cooked foods at street stalls should be avoided; fruit and vegetables should be peeled or thoroughly cleaned and cooked. Take care with shellfish, eggs and salads. Eat at busy, clean premises. Wear sunscreen and a hat when out in the sun. Bring your own contraceptives, tampons and sunscreen.

Pharmacies

Pharmacies (*nha thuoc*) are well stocked, selling imported drugs, although there is a big problem with fake and expired drugs (check sell-by dates and packaging) and bogus pharmacists. Bring your own medications and first-aid kit. **Hanoi Family Medical Practice** and **International SOS** (*see below*) have the most reliable pharmacies: better local pharmacies are at 2 Hang Bai, 48 Hai Ba Trung and 3 Trang Thi streets.

Medical/Dental Services

Buy comprehensive medical insurance *before* you go to Vietnam.

Right: Hanoi police officers

Hanoi French Hospital, 1 Phuong Mai Street, tel: 04-574 0740; emergencies tel: 04-574 1111; www.hfh.com.vn. International standard foreign-invested hospital, with French and Vietnamese doctors on duty. Its facilities include a 24-hour accident and emergency ward, operating theatre, intensive care and general admission wards, and a dental clinic.

International SOS, Central Building, 31 Hai Ba Trung Street, tel: 04-934 0666; emergencies tel: 04-934 0556; www.internationalsos.com. Medical and dental clinic staffed by multilingual expatriate and local team of healthcare professionals providing 24-hour international-standard care. Emergency and full medical evacuation services.

Hanoi Family Medical Practice, Building A1, Room 109–122, Van Phuc Compound, Kim Ma Road, tel: 04-843 0748; emergencies tel: 0903 401 919; www. vietnammedicalpractice.com. First and only 100 percent foreign-invested and managed private international health clinic, with multi-national doctors. Facilities include 24-hour emergency service, in-patient and intensive care facilities, medical evacuation and dental clinic (tel: 04-823 0281).

Crime/Trouble

Vietnam is acknowledged as one of the safest tourist destinations in the world (especially for women). Violent crimes against foreigners are extremely rare; penalties for harming a foreigner are severe. Hanoi is one of the safest cities in the world and unlike Ho Chi Minh City, there are few occurrences of bag snatching and petty crimes involving foreigners. But this does not mean that you should let your guard down. Always store valuables in hotel safes. When out, keep cash and documents in a concealed money belt, keep a firm hand on your possessions (especially when using public transport) and don't dress ostentatiously: jewellery, cameras, bags, etc, are magnets for drive-by motorbike thieves. Take extra care when travelling on local transport at night.

Noise

Vietnam is an incredibly noisy place from dawn to around 10pm, when locals retire. Building work, karaoke rooms and early morning (and afternoon) communal loudspeaker broadcasts are culprits. A Hanoi peculiarity is the constant honking of vehicle horns, even when it's totally unnecessary. Bring earplugs and a sense of humour.

Police

The police are instructed not to hassle foreigners, so as not to upset the tourism trade. But foreigners are still viewed with suspicion and activities may be monitored by undercover security police. In accordance with Vietnamese law, when you check-in at a hotel, you must present your passport and landing card and fill in a form. This information is then sent to the police for registration purposes.

COMMUNICATIONS & NEWS

Post

Post offices (*buu dien*) open daily, from 6–7am, closing 8.30–10pm. The main **GPO** is at 75 Dien Tien Hoang Street: here you can send parcels (Mon–Sat 7.30am–noon, 1–4.30pm), letters, faxes and make overseas or domestic calls. Sub-branches are at 66 Luong Van Can Street, 66–68 Trang Tien Street and Hanoi Towers, 49 Hai Ba Trung Street.

Telephones

Coin-operated pay phones are being introduced at post offices and public outlets; most public phones require phonecards (for domestic or international use) – available at the post office. Even though charges are falling, costs of overseas calls from Vietnam remain the highest in the world.

To call overseas from Vietnam, dial 00, followed by the country code, area code, then local number. Using the prefixes 171, 178 or 177 before the international access code 00 saves money on overseas and long-distance domestic calls – certain conditions apply.

Cheapest rates are phones using the Internet, found in Internet cafés.

Note: hotels add hefty charges for making overseas calls or sending faxes.

Mobile Telephones

Only users of GSM mobile phones with global roaming service can connect automatically with Vietnam's network. Check with your service provider at home if not sure, especially if coming from Japan or the US, which uses a different network system altogether. To save on expensive phone charges, buy a local SIM card and pre-paid phonecards in Hanoi.

Note: mobile phone numbers in Vietnam begin with 09.

Useful Phone Numbers

Hanoi country code: 84
Hanoi area code: 04
Operator: 110
Police: 113
Fire: 114
Enquiries: 116
Medical emergencies: 115

Business Centres and Internet

Hanoi has limited business facilities and quality Internet cafés. All top-end hotels have business centres, or try the **Press Club**, 59a Ly Thai To Street, tel: 04-934 0888. Many hotels have Internet access; there are numerous Internet cafés around town. Rates are very cheap but service can be slow.

Media and Publications

Hanoi isn't that well stocked with international magazines and newspapers; try top-end hotels, the **Press Club** (*address above*); **Xunhasaba**, 32 Hai Ba Trung Street; and **Thang Long Bookshop**, 53–55 Trang Tien Street. English-language newspapers include

Vietnam News, Vietnam Investment Review and *Vietnam Economic Times*.

For English-language books, try **Savina**, 44 Trang Tien Street; the **Press Club**; and **Bookworm**, 15a Ngo Van So Street – Hanoi's only English bookstore.

VOV5 (FM 105.5MHz) – part of the government-run Voice of Vietnam radio – has English broadcasts five times a day. Many hotels provide satellite TV, however transmissions can be limited or erratic.

LANGUAGE

Vietnamese is tonal and very difficult to learn. A Romanised script (*quoc ngu*) is used. Variations in dialect, accent and pronunciation exist between Hanoi and elsewhere; northern minority groups have their own languages. English is increasingly spoken in tourist-orientated outlets and by the young.

The syllable is the language's base unit and each can be pronounced in six different tones to convey six meanings. For example the syllable '*bo*' can mean a children's toilet, father, lover, to chop, impolite, or a government ministry. Obviously that leaves much room for confusion for any novice and anyone on the receiving end of a beginner's efforts!

Basic Phrases

The basic hello – *chao*, is always followed by another word that varies depending on the age and sex of whom you address.

for an old lady/*Chao ba*
for a young lady/*Chao co*
for an older lady/*Chao chi*
for an old man/*Chao ong*
for a young man/*Chao anh*
for an older man/*Chao bac*
for a young person/*Chao em*
goodbye/*Tam biet*
See you again/*Hen gap lai*
I am sorry/*Xin loi*
Please/*xin moi*
thank you/*cam on*
yes/*da*
no/*khong*

O dau?/where? comes at the end of the sentence directly after the noun. For example, if you want to ask for the post office – *Buu dien o dau?*

USEFUL INFORMATION

Disabled

Disabled accessibility is poor, not helped by traffic, congested pavements, lack of lifts and ramps, and old infrastructure. However, things are changing with increased wealth, tourism, Vietnam's recent hosting of the ASEAN Para Games and a government approved Barrier-Free Access Building Code and Standards. Generally new, high-end or larger establishments are wheelchair accessible (as is Hanoi Airport); but some smaller hotels are now investing in lifts and larger rooms.

Vietnam Disability Forum supplies information about disabled facilities, at http://forum.wso.net.

Children

Foreign children get a huge amount of attention everywhere they go in Vietnam. The main childcare concerns are health and hygiene aspects, congested pavements, traffic and humid summers. However, journey times across the city are relatively short and there are many parks available. Public swimming pools are poorly maintained; stick to hotel facilities.

Supermarkets

Intimex: 22–32 Le Thai To Street
Western Canned Food: 66 Ba Trieu Street
Vinacomex: Trang Tien Plaza, Trang Tien Street
Trade Centre: 7 Dinh Tien Hoang Street
Citimart: Hanoi Towers, 49 Hai Ba Trung Street; Vincom City Tower, 191 Ba Trieu Street.

Tourist Information/Maps

Vietnam's tourism industry lags behind other Asian countries. Even in the capital, you won't find official tourist information kiosks giving out impartial free information. The official representative and responsibility for Vietnam's tourism – domestically and overseas – comes under the government-run **Vietnam National Administration of Tourism** (VNAT; www.vietnamtourism.com), which is more involved in new hotels and infrastructure investments than in providing tourist services. State-run 'tourist offices' under the VNAT (or local provincial organi-

Left: Hanoi's main post office, Buu Dien Ha Noi

sations) are merely tour agents who are out to make money and are not geared to Western requirements. For tours, car hire, information, go to private-run tour agencies, but use established, reliable outfits (*see below*).

Maps are obtainable from book stores on Trang Tien Street, from street kids, or hotel receptions. Hanoi tourist information, maps and listings are found in English-language magazines: *Vietnam Discovery, Vietnam Pathfinder, The Guide* (*Vietnam Economic Times* supplement), *Time Out* (*Vietnam Investment Review* supplement) and *Vietnam Heritage* (Vietnam Airlines in-flight magazine).

Call **1080** for a state-run, telephone information service – with English-speaking staff.

Tour Operators
Buffalo Tours
11 Hang Muoi Street
Tel: 04-828 0702; Fax: 04-826 9370
www.buffalotours.com
Established in 1994, this Vietnamese privately-owned company offers quality scheduled and customised tours for adventure, luxury or corporate travel, plus the usual travel services. Experienced, knowledgeable guides with an emphasis on low-impact tourism.

Compagnie Bourlingue
51 Cua Dong Street
Tel: 04-747 0545; Fax: 04-747 0557
www.freewheelin-tours.com
Reliable French-Vietnamese outfit runs customised Minsk motorbike tours and treks in remote regions of the north. Guides have in-depth knowledge of the area and minorities.

Exotissimo
26 Tran Nhat Duat Street
Tel: 04-828 2150; Fax: 04-928 0056
www.exotissimo.com
The first-joint venture tour company, this efficient outfit offers quality tailor-made and scheduled tours, travel services and adventure trips. Prices are higher than other Hanoi tour operators, but reliability and good service are its hallmarks.

Explore Indochina
Rm. 500, Tuoi Tre Hotel
2 Tran Thanh Tong Street
Tel: 091 352 4658
www.exploreindochina.com
Expert expatriates with in-depth regional knowledge run tailor-made, off-the-beaten track Minsk motorbiking tours in the north. Caters for all levels of drivers; small group tours.

Handspan Adventure Travel
80 Ma May Street
Tel: 04-926 0581
www.handspan.com
Established in 1997, this is a young adventure travel company that offers excellent value-for-money tours such as kayaking, mountain biking, trekking and cruising, with experienced guides and an environmentally sensitive focus.

Hidden Hanoi
5 Ngo 142, Au Co Street
Tel: 091 225 4045
www.hiddenhanoi.com
Organises in-depth and small-group cultural and culinary tours of Hanoi (walking tours, plus Vietnamese cooking and language classes) all led by local experts.

Topas
20 Cau May Street, Sapa
Tel: 020-871331; Fax: 020-871596, and
29 Hang Giay Street, Hanoi
Tel: 04-928 3637; Fax: 04-928 3638
www.topas-adventure-vietnam.com
High-end joint Danish-Vietnamese company specialising in tailor-made itineraries – especially adventure – in Sapa and the north. Emphasis on low-impact and eco-friendly tours, with quality service.

Above: Halong Bay is best seen on an overnight boat trip

ACKNOWLEDGEMENTS

Front Cover	**Kevin R. Morris/Corbis**
Back Cover (top)	**Julian Abram Wainwright**
Back Cover (bottom)	**Exotissimo**
Photography	
2/3, 5T, 6C/B, 7B, 8/9, 16, 22T, 24T, 25, 27, 31B, 33, 34T/B, 36T/B, 39T/B, 40, 41, 42T/B, 43, 45, 46, 47, 48T/B, 49, 50, 51, 52, 53T/B, 54, 55, 56, 57, 58, 59, 60, 61, 62T, 63, 64T/B, 65, 66, 67, 71B, 72, 73, 76, 77, 78, 80, 81, 83, 84, 85, 87, 95, 98	**Julian Abram Wainwright/APA**
1, 5B, 6T, 7T, 11, 15, 20, 21, 22B, 23, 24B, 28, 29, 30, 31T, 32T/B, 35, 44, 62B, 71T, 75, 79, 86, 88, 89, 91, 92, 97	**Jim Holmes/APA**
10, 14, 70	**Catherine Karnow**
69	**Emeraude Classic Cruises**
68T/B, 100	**Exotissimo**
12	**Pierre Dieulefils**
37, 80	**Sofitel Metrople**
13	**Vietnam News Agency**
Cartography	**Mapping Ideas Ltd**

© APA Publications GmbH & Co. Verlag KG Singapore Branch, Singapore

INDEX